The Attributes of God Volume 1
with Study Guide

A.W. TOZER

The ATTRIBUTES of GOD

VOLUME 1

A Journey Into the Father's Heart

WITH STUDY GUIDE

by
DAVID FESSENDEN

WingSpread Publishers
Chicago, Illinois

$\mathcal{W}$ing$\mathcal{S}$pread $\mathcal{P}$ublishers
Chicago, Illinois

www.moodypublishers.com

An imprint of Moody Publishers

The Attributes of God Volume 1 with Study Guide
ISBN: 978-1-60066-129-7
LOC Catalog Card Number: 2006936041
Attributes of God Volume 1 © 1997
by The Moody Bible Institute of Chicago
Attributes of God Volume 1 Study Guide © 2003
by David E. Fessenden

Previously published by Christian Publications, Inc.
First Christian Publications edition 2003
First WingSpread Publishers edition 2007
The Attributes of God was first published
by Christian Publications in 1997.
The Study Guide was added in 2003.

Cover design by Design Source Creative Services

10

Scripture taken from
The Holy Bible: King James Version.

Contents

Chapter 1

God's Infinitude

If ye then be risen with Christ, seek those things which are above, where Christ sitteth on the right hand of God. Set your affection on things above, not on things on the earth. For ye are dead, and your life is hid with Christ in God. (Colossians 3:1-3)

The last eight words of this verse would make a good sermon for anybody: "Your life is hid with Christ in God." I want to go to a book written six hundred years ago and quote a few things, weaving it into this message about the journey into the heart of God: "with Christ in God."

The Journey to Infinity

This book was written by Lady Julian of Norwich, a very saintly woman.

I want to quote what this lady said about the Trinity: "Suddenly the Trinity filled my heart with

1

joy. And I understood that so it shall be in heaven without end." This is a step up from the utilitarian heaven that most people want to go to, where they'll have everything right—a split-level home, two cars and a fountain, a swimming pool and golden streets. Lady Julian saw that heaven will be heaven because the Trinity will fill our hearts with "joy without end," for the Trinity is God and God is the Trinity. The Trinity is our Maker and Keeper, and the Trinity is our everlasting love and everlasting joy and bliss.

All these things marked Jesus Christ, and, as Julian said, "where Jesus appeareth the blessed Trinity is understood." We must get into our heads and hearts that Jesus Christ is the full, complete manifestation of the Trinity: "He that hath seen me hath seen the Father" (John 14:9). He set forth the glory of the Triune God, all the God there is! Where Jesus appears, God is. And where Jesus is glorified, God is.

I wouldn't quote anybody unless there were Scripture to confirm it, and Scripture does indeed confirm that the Trinity will fill our hearts. "No man hath seen God at any time. If we love one another, God dwelleth in us, and his love is perfected in us. Hereby know we that we dwell in him, and he in us, because he hath given us of his Spirit" (1 John 4:12-13). There you have the Father and the Spirit. "And we have seen and do testify that the Father sent the Son to be the Saviour of the world. Whosoever shall confess that Jesus is the Son of God, God dwelleth in him, and he in

God" (4:14-15). There you have the Father and the Son, or the Trinity.

"Neither pray I for these alone, but for them also which shall believe on me through their word; that they all may be one; as thou, Father, art in me, and I in thee, that they also may be one in us: that the world may believe that thou hast sent me" (John 17:20-21). Do you believe on Jesus Christ through the word of the apostles? If you do, then Jesus said distinctly here, "I'm praying for you that you all may be one as the Father is in me and I in him, that you may be one in us. I in you and the Father in me."

The other day I heard a man pray this prayer: "Oh God, who art the truth, make me one with Thee in everlasting love. It wearieth me often to read and hear many things, but in Thee is all that I would have and can desire." The Church will come out of her doldrums when we find out that salvation is not a lightbulb only, that it is not an insurance policy against hell only, but that it is a gateway into God and that God is all that we would have and can desire. Again I quote Julian: "I saw that God is to us everything that is good and comfortable. He is our clothing; His love wrappeth us and claspeth us and all encloseth us for His tender love, that He may never leave us, being to us all that is good."

Christianity is a gateway into God. And then when you get into God, "with Christ in God," then you're on a journey into infinity, into infinitude. There is no limit and no place to stop. There isn't just one work of grace, or a second work or a third work, and then that's it. There are *numberless* experiences and spiritual epochs and crises that can take place in your life while you are journeying out into the heart of God in Christ.

God is infinite! That's the hardest thought I will ask you to grasp. You cannot understand what infinite means, but don't let it bother you—I don't understand it and I'm trying to explain it! "Infinite" means so much that nobody can grasp it, but reason nevertheless kneels and acknowledges that God is infinite. We mean by infinite that God knows no limits, no bounds and no end. What God is, He is without boundaries. All that God is, He is without bounds or limits.

Infinity Cannot Be Measured

We've got to eliminate all careless speech here. You and I talk about unlimited wealth, but there's no such thing; you can count it. We talk about boundless energy—which I don't feel I have at the moment—but there's no such thing; you can measure a man's energy. We say an artist takes infinite pains with his picture. But he doesn't take infinite pains; he just does the best he can and then throws up his hands and says, "It isn't right yet, but I'll have to let it go." That's what we call infinite pains.

But that is a misuse of the words "boundless," "unlimited" and "infinite." These words describe God—they don't describe anything *but* God. They do not describe space or time or matter or motion or energy; these words do not apply to creatures or sand or stars or anything that can be measured.

Measurement is a way created things have of accounting for themselves. Weight, for instance, is one way we account for ourselves—by the gravitational pull of the earth. And then we have distance—space between heavenly bodies. Then we have length—extension of the body into space.

We can always measure things. We know how big the sun is, how big the moon is, how much the earth weighs, how much the sun and other heavenly bodies weigh. We know approximately how much water is in the ocean. It seems boundless to us, but we know how deep it is and we can measure it, so it really isn't boundless at all. There is nothing boundless but God and nothing infinite but God. God is self-existent and absolute; everything else is contingent and relative. There is nothing very big and nothing very wise and nothing very wonderful. It's all relatively so. It is only God who knows no degrees.

The poet says, "One God, one Majesty. There is no God but Thee. Unbounded, unextended unity." For a long time I wondered why he said, "unbounded, *unextended* unity"; then I realized he meant that God doesn't *extend* into space; God *contains* space. C.S. Lewis said that if you could think of a sheet of paper infinitely extended in all directions, and if you took a pencil and made a line one inch long on it, that would be time. When you started to push your pencil it was the beginning of time and when you lifted it off the paper it was the end of time. And all around, infinitely extended in all directions, is God. That's a good illustration.

If there were a point where God stopped, then God wouldn't be perfect. For instance, if God knew almost everything, but not quite everything, then God wouldn't be perfect in knowledge. His understanding wouldn't be infinite, as it says in Psalm 147:5.

Let us take all that can be known—past, present and future, spiritual, psychic and physical—everywhere throughout the universe. And let us say God knows all of it except one percent—He knows ninety-nine percent of all that can be known. I'd be embarrassed to go to heaven and look into the face of a God that didn't know *everything*. He has to know it all or I can't worship Him. I can't worship that which is not perfect.

What about power? If God had all the power there is except a little bit, and if somebody else had a little bit of power hoarded that God couldn't get to, then we couldn't worship God. We couldn't say that this God is of infinite power because He wouldn't be of infinite power; He'd just be close to it. While He would be more powerful than any other being and perhaps even more powerful than all the beings in the universe lumped together, He still would have a defect, and therefore He couldn't be God. Our God is perfect—perfect in knowledge and power.

If God had goodness, but there was one spot in God that wasn't good, then He wouldn't be our

God and Father. If God had love but didn't have *all* the love, just ninety-nine and nine-tenths percent of the love—or even a higher percentage—God still wouldn't be God. God, to *be* God, must be infinite in all that He is. He must have no bound and no limit, no stopping place, no point beyond which He can't go. When you think of God or anything about God you'll have to think infinitely about God.

You may have a charley horse in your head for two weeks after trying to follow this, but it's a mighty good cure for this little cheap god we have today. This little cheap god we've made up is one you can pal around with—"the Man upstairs," the fellow who helps you win baseball games. That god isn't the God of Abraham, Isaac and Jacob. He isn't the God who laid the foundations of the heaven and the earth; he's some other god.

We educated Americans can create gods just the same as the heathen can. You can make a god out of silver or wood or stone—or you can make it out of your own imagination. And the god that's being worshiped in many places is simply a god of imagination. He's not the true God. He's not the infinite, perfect, all-knowing, all-wise, all-loving, infinitely boundless, perfect God. He's something short of that. Christianity is decaying and going down into the gutter because the god of modern Christianity is not the God of the Bible. I don't mean to say that we do not pray to God; I mean to say that we pray to a god short of what he ought to be. We have got to think of God as being the perfect One.

God Takes Pleasure in Himself

The next thing I am about to say may give you a little shock: God takes pleasure in Himself and rejoices in His own perfection. I've prayed and thought and searched and read the Word too long to ever take that back. God takes pleasure in Himself and He rejoices in His own perfection. The divine Trinity is glad in Himself! God delights in His works.

When God created the heaven and the earth and all things that are upon the earth, He kept saying, "It was good" (Genesis 1:4, 10, 12, 18, 21, 25). Then when God created man in His own image He looked and said, "It was very good" (1:31). God rejoiced in His works. He was glad in what He had done.

Redemption is not a heavy work for God. God didn't find Himself in a fix and have to rush off somewhere and try to get "foreign policy" straightened out with the archangels. God did what He did joyfully. He made the heaven and the earth joyfully. That's why the flowers look up and smile, and the birds sing and the sun shines, and the sky is blue and rivers trickle down to the sea. God made the creation and He loved what He did!

He took pleasure in Himself, in His own perfection and in the perfection of His work. And when it comes to redemption, I repeat that this was not a heavy task laid upon God by moral necessity. God wanted to do this. There was no moral necessity upon God to redeem mankind. He didn't have to send His Son Jesus Christ to die for mankind. He sent Him, but at the same time Jesus did it voluntarily. If God was willing, it was the happy willingness of God.

A mother doesn't have to get up and feed her baby at 2 in the morning. There's no law compelling her to do it. The law probably would compel her to take some care of the little tyke, but she doesn't have to give him that loving care that she does. She wants to do it. I used to do it for our little fellows, and I enjoyed doing it. A mother and a father do what they do because they love to do it.

It is the same with this awesome, eternal, invisible, infinite, all-wise, omniscient God, the God of our fathers, the God and Father of our Lord Jesus Christ and the God we call "our Father which art in heaven." He is boundless and infinite; He can't be weighed or measured; you can't apply distance or time or space to Him, for He made it all and contains it all in His own heart. While He rises above it all, at the same time this God is a friendly, congenial God, and He delights in Himself. The Father delights in the Son: "This is my beloved Son, in whom I am well pleased" (Matthew 3:17). The Son delighted in the Father: "I thank thee, O Father, Lord of heaven and earth" (Matthew 11:25). And certainly the Holy Ghost delights in the Father and the Son.

The incarnation, too, was not something that Jesus Christ did gritting His teeth and saying, "I hate this thing—I wish I could get out of it." One of the dear old hymn writers said, "He abhorred not the virgin's womb." The writer thought about this and said, "Wait a minute here. The womb of the creature? How could the everlasting, eternal, infinite God, whom space cannot contain, confine Himself inside one of His creatures? Wouldn't it be a humiliation?" Then he smiled and said, "No, He abhorred not the virgin's womb," and he wrote it and we've been singing it for centuries. The incarnation of Jesus Christ's immortal flesh was not a heavy thing. The second person of the Trinity, the everlasting Son, the eternal Word made Himself flesh—joyously! When the angels sang about the incarnation, they sang joyously about it.

God Takes Pleasure in His Work

And He also delights in salvation. Notice in Luke 15:5 that when Jesus Christ saves a man, He carries him on His shoulders. And what is the verb in that verse? It is *rejoicing!* God is not only pleased with Himself, delighted with His own perfection and happy in His work of creating and redeeming, but He is also enthusiastic. There is an enthusiasm in the Godhead, and there is enthusiasm in creation.

If there weren't enthusiasm in creation, it would soon run down. Everything is made of atoms, protons, neutrons and electrons, things you can't keep still—not for a second! They dash in all directions at tremendous speeds, and the heavenly bodies move the same way.

The old Greeks called the movement they made as they passed through space "the music of the

spheres." I don't think they've missed it by very
much at all. I believe that God sang when He created things. The motion and speed of the heavenly bodies, the working of little creatures in the
earth to make the soil soft, the working of the sun
on the earth—all this is God joyously working in
His creation.

Enthusiasm is seen in creation; it's seen in light.
Did you ever stop to think what it would be like if
there were no light? If God Almighty were to put
a lead sack around all the heavenly bodies and
suddenly shut out all the light there is, I wouldn't
want to be alive. I would want to turn myself off
like a light bulb and ask God please to annihilate
me—and I don't believe in annihilation. Imagine:
no light, no speed, no color or sound!

Some people are afraid of color. They think that
spirituality consists in being drab. But God made
color! He made all shades of colors. Look at the
sunset—what is it, just something scientific? Do
you think that God splashed the lovely, beautiful
sky with rose, cerise, blue and white and wasn't
smiling when He did that? Is that just an accident
of nature, scientifically explained? Then you've
got too much learning for your own good! Go
empty your head and get your heart filled and
you'll be better off. The Holy Spirit wrote 150
psalms and in those psalms He celebrates the
wonders of God's creation.

In my state of Pennsylvania the money-greedy
scoundrels have bought the coal rights in certain
sections of the state. There were beautiful hills

there that I grew up to see and love, beautiful sun-kissed hills sometimes mystic blue in the setting of the sun. And the creeks ran below out to the rivers and down to the sea. It was all very beautiful.

But I went back to my old place years later, and I found that these money-hungry fellows didn't dig a hole to get the coal; they took bulldozers and dragged the top off the earth—trees, grass, everything—to get down to the coal. The result was that thousands and thousands of acres—whole hills that used to go up with their green to meet heaven's blue—lay gashed like one vast, gaping grave. The state of Pennsylvania said, "You've got to fill them all in or we'll fine you $300." And the mining people looked at each other and grinned and paid the $300. They left it as it was, and I went away grief-stricken to see my beautiful hills now great ugly sand pits.

I went back in a few more years, and do you know what nature had done? Dear old busy, enthusiastic, fun-loving, joyous Mother Nature began to draw a green veil over that ugly gash. And now if you go back you will see it has cured itself. It's God Almighty in that! We ought to stop thinking like scientists and think like psalmists.

This infinite God is enjoying Himself. Somebody is having a good time in heaven and earth and sea and sky. Somebody is painting the sky. Somebody is making trees to grow where only gashes were a year ago. Somebody is causing the ice to melt out of the river and the fish to swim and the birds to

sing and lay their blue eggs and build their nests
and hatch their young. Somebody's running the
universe.

Singing for Joy

And I believe I know who it is. I believe it is the
eternal Father, "strong to save, whose power rules
the restless wave." I believe it is the Trinity, our
Father who art in heaven and Jesus Christ His
only Son our Lord. God is having a good time in
His role. And so let us not think anymore of God
as being heavy-browed and gloomy. I repeat that
when God made the heaven and earth they sang
together and all the sons of God shouted for joy.
There wasn't a funeral at the creation of the
world; there was an anthem. All creation sang.

At the incarnation they sang. Some people put a
clammy, pasty pall over your happy mouths and
say, "The angels didn't *sing*, `peace on earth, good
will to men.' According to the Greek, they *said*,
`peace on earth, good will to men.' " But you can't
read that without something beginning to move in
you. You get a rhythm; you get music in your
heart. "Peace on earth, good will toward men,"
they said. There was singing at the incarnation.

And then at the resurrection there was singing.
"I will sing unto thee among the nations" (Psalm
57:9) said Jesus in the psalm. It doesn't tell us in
the New Testament that Jesus sang when He rose
from the dead. But the Old Testament foretells
that one of the first things Jesus would do was
sing. And one of the last things He did before He

went out to die was to sing a hymn along with His brethren. I'd love to have heard that hymn!

Did you ever stop to think about the rapture? It's going to be something that's never happened before. You might be walking around on the street and hear the sound of the trumpet—and suddenly you're transformed! You won't know what to do or how to act. And the people lying in their graves, what'll they do? I know what they'll do—they'll sing! There's going to be singing at the consummation, on that great day!

"Thou art worthy to take the book, and to open the seals thereof: for thou wast slain, and hast redeemed us" (Revelation 5:9)—that's the theme of the new song. The theme of the new song isn't "I am"; it's "Thou art." Notice the difference! When you look at the old hymnody of Wesley, Montgomery and Watts, it was "Thou art, O God, Thou art." But when you look at the modern hymns, it is "I am, I am, I am." It makes me sick to my stomach. Occasionally a good hymn with testimonies is all right, but we've overdone it. The song of the ransomed is going to be "Thou art worthy, O God."

> And they sung a new song, saying, Thou art worthy to take the book, and to open the seals thereof: for thou wast slain, and hast redeemed us to God by thy blood out of every kindred, and tongue, and people, and nation; and hast made us unto our God kings and priests: and we shall reign on the

earth. And I beheld, and I heard the voice of
many angels round about the throne and the
beasts and the elders: and the number of
them was ten thousand times ten thousand,
and thousands of thousands. (Revelation
5:9-11)

If you can put on a blackboard how many that
is, I'll buy you dinner. Isn't it strange that men
have got such timber in their heads that instead of
getting happy over this they solemnly try to figure
out who these deacons and elders and beasts and
creatures were? And they write books on who
they were and what they looked like. Isn't that
strange? How dumb can a scholar get? I don't
know about these creatures here. See me five minutes after the rapture and I'll tell you about it. But
now I'll just have to take it by faith. "Thou hast
made us . . . kings and priests," John said. All the
creatures said, "Worthy is the Lamb" (5:12). Not
"Look at me. I am wonderful; I am happy, happy,
happy." No—the Lamb, the Lamb is worthy.
    That's the consummation. The infinite God-
head invites us into Himself to share in all the in-
timacies of the Trinity. And Christ is the way in.
    The moon and earth turn in such a way that we
only see one side of the moon and never see the
other. The eternal God is so vast, so infinite, that I
can't hope to know all about God and all there is
about God. But God has a manward side, just as
the moon has an earthward side. Just as the moon
always keeps that smiling yellow face turned

earthward, so God has a side He always keeps turned manward, and that side is Jesus Christ. Jesus Christ is God's manward face. Earth's Godward side, Jesus, is the way God sees us. He always looks down and sees us in Jesus Christ. Then we go back to the quotation from Lady Julian: "Where Jesus appeareth the blessed Trinity is understood."

Are you contented with nominal Christianity? If you are, I've nothing for you. Are you contented with popular Christianity that runs on the authority and popularity of big shots? If you are, I've nothing for you. Are you content with elementary Christianity? If you are, all I've got for you is to exhort you earnestly to press on toward perfection. But if you're not satisfied with nominal Christianity, popular Christianity and the first beginnings of things and you want to know the Triune God for yourself, read on.

Chapter 2

God's Immensity

For whosoever will save his life shall lose it: and whosoever will lose his life for my sake shall find it. For what is a man profited, if he shall gain the whole world, and lose his own soul? (Matthew 16:25-26)

And your life is hid with Christ in God. (Colossians 3:3)

Yea doubtless, and I count all things but loss for the excellency of the knowledge of Christ Jesus my Lord: for whom I have suffered the loss of all things, and do count them but dung, that I may win Christ. (Philippians 3:8)

Father, we're unworthy to think these thoughts, and our friends are unworthy to hear them expressed. But we will try to hear worthily and speak worthily. We know that we

*have looked upon evil sights, heard with our
ears evil words and walked in evil ways. But
now we trust that is behind us and our eyes
are upon Thee. Show Thyself to us, O God!
Shepherd, sweet Wonder, Jesus, we ask You
now that this evening we may again have a vision of the triune God through Jesus Christ our
Lord. Amen.*

Faith is of two kinds: nominal and real. The
nominal faith is faith that accepts what it is
told and can quote text after text to prove it.
It's amazing how nominal faith and nominal belief
can weave these texts into garments, cloaks and
curtains for the Church.

But there is another kind of faith: it is faith that
depends upon the character of God. You will remember that the Scripture does not say, "Abraham believed *the text*, and it was counted unto
him for righteousness." It says, "Abraham believed *God*" (Romans 4:3). It was not *what* Abraham believed, it was *who* Abraham believed that
counted. Abraham believed God, and the man of
true faith believes God and his faith rests on the
character of God. The man who has real faith
rather than nominal faith has found a right answer to the question, "What is God like?" There is
no question more important. The man of true
faith has found an answer to that question by revelation and illumination.

The difficulty with the Church now—even the
Bible-believing Church—is that we stop with

revelation. But revelation is not enough. Revelation is God's given Word. It's an objective thing, not subjective; it's external, not internal. It is God's revelation of truth. A man may believe that and believe it soundly and hold it to be truth. And yet he will have only an objective revelation of truth that has been objectively revealed.

Illumination

There is another way to find an answer to the question, "What is God like?" and that is by illumination. The man of real faith believes the Word, but it has been illuminated so that he knows what the Word means. That doesn't mean that he's a better Bible teacher. But it means that he has had what the Quakers call "an opening." His heart has been opened to the Word. The given revelation is a means toward an end, and God is the end, not the text itself.

That's why I never fight over a translation and get all worked up and steamed up over it. A text is a means to an end. Now, since there's plenty of money and the printers will print anything, we're making the mistake of thinking that if we get the Word said in a different way there'll be some magic effect in that Word. We think that if it is read in the King James Version that's OK, but if we get a new version, varying just a little, we have automatically received something new. It doesn't follow!

The illumination is what matters and the Word of God is a means toward an end, just as roads are means toward destinations. A road is nothing in itself. Nobody ever built a road and fenced it in at both ends and planted posies along it and beautified it and said, "This is a road." They said, "This is a way, a means toward somewhere." The Bible is a whole series of highways, all leading toward God. And when the text has been illuminated and the believer of the text knows that God is the end toward which he is moving, then that man has real faith.

The Size of Things

I speak often of a little book called *The Revelation of the Divine Love* written by a woman by the name of Julian six hundred years ago. One day as she prayed she had a little experience, and here's what it was. She said, "I saw a very small object as large as a hazelnut." When I was a boy on the farm we had hazelnuts, and hazelnuts as we knew them were about the size of a large marble, no larger than that. She said she saw this little tiny object, and she asked, "What might this be?" And something in her heart said, "This is all that is made; this is all that is made." This little tiny hazelnut-sized affair is all that is made. I want you to think about this with me: "This is all that is made."

The great French philosopher and mystic mathematician, Pascal, said this: "We are halfway between immensity and that which is infinitesimally small." He said you will find worlds beyond worlds out in space. Our solar system moves around another solar system. And that solar system moves around another solar system, and so on into infinite vastness. Then, he said, if you turn the other way, you will find little worlds within little worlds going down—the molecule, the atom, the electron and the proton, down into infinitesimal smallness. He believed that man, made in the image of God, is exactly halfway in between that which is infinitely large and that which is infinitesimally small. There is no way to prove that, but that's a frightening place to be, half as big as the universe but also half as small.

We think that the sun is very large with its planets circling around it. But if you study astronomy—even elementary astronomy—you will learn that there are suns so large that each one could absorb our sun, all of its planets and all of the satellites that revolve around those planets into itself. They say that there are suns that are so large you could put millions of our suns into them. I give up. I don't even try to understand it.

Then there is space. I don't think space is a thing; I think it is just a way we have of accounting for different positions in the vast universe. We call it distance. We know they don't measure it. If it's the moon they say 250,000 miles or if it's the sun they say 93 million miles. But after that they start talking in light years. They say that there are bodies millions of light years away—say 10 million just to get a start. So if you want to know how far it is from earth to that body I'm talking about, you multiply 5 trillion, 862 billion, 484 million by 10 million. Doesn't that stun you? It makes my head ache! Seen over against this, you and I are terribly small.

Now we're not the smallest thing there is, because you can dissolve us, melt us down and get at the molecules and atoms and bits of disembodied matter or energy that we call by various manufactured names. You'll find that we're, according to Pascal, half as big as the universe.

The Immanence of God

Then there is God. God has the attribute of immanence and immensity. God is immanent, which means you don't have to go distances to find God. He is in everything. He is right here.

God is above all things, beneath all things, outside of all things and inside of all things. God is above, but He's not pushed up. He's beneath, but He's not pressed down. He's outside, but He's not excluded. He's inside, but He's not confined. God is above all things presiding, beneath all things sustaining, outside of all things embracing and inside of all things filling. That is the immanence of God.

God doesn't travel to get anywhere. We may say in prayer, "Oh God, come and help us," because we mean it in a psychological way. But actually God doesn't have to "come" to help us because *there isn't any place where God is not.*

> If I take the wings of the morning, and
> dwell in the uttermost parts of the sea; even
> there shall thy hand lead me, and thy right

hand shall hold me. . . . If I ascend up into heaven, thou art there: if I make my bed in hell, behold, thou art there. (Psalm 139:9-10, 8)

So it's impossible to think of a place where God is not.

The Immensity of God

The Scripture also teaches the immensity of God. It says in Isaiah, "Who hath measured the waters in the hollow of his hand, and meted out heaven with the span, and comprehended the dust of the earth in a measure, and weighed the mountains in scales, and the hills in a balance?" (40:12).

Imagine going out millions of light years into space and finding a body so vast that you could throw all our solar system into it. Like throwing a shovelful of coal into a furnace, it would simply swallow up our solar system and go on. After you've thought of all that, remember that God contains all that. Remember that God is outside of all things and inside of all things and around all things. Remember that our God made it. That is the immensity of God.

The Holy Ghost is bigger than all the universe, this little hazelnut that Julian saw. "Behold, the nations are as a drop of a bucket" (40:15). You know, it's awfully hard to get a Christian scared. It's hard to get him panicked if he really believes in God. If he's just a church member, you can get

him panicked. But if he really believes in God it's
very difficult to do it.

It's very difficult for a big-mouth like Nikita
Khrushchev [leader of the former Soviet Union in
the 1950s and 1960s] to scare anybody who really
believes in God. Khrushchev is beginning to sound
more and more like Adolf Hitler—and where is
Hitler? The same God who disposed of Adolf can
dispose of Nikita one of these days. "Behold, the
nations are as a drop of a bucket, and are counted
as the small dust of the balance: behold, he taketh
up the isles as a very little thing" (40:15)—so small
He doesn't even notice them. "All nations before
him are as nothing; and they are counted to him
less than nothing, and vanity" (40:17).

Old Dr. Neighbor used to say that the word
vanity in the Hebrew meant "a soap bubble"—something that floats along on an infinitesimally thin skin. You touch it and it's gone; no one
can find it again. That's what it means: all the nations of the world are to Him as a soap bubble.

It is he that sitteth upon the circle of the
earth, and the inhabitants thereof are as
grasshoppers; that stretcheth out the heavens as a curtain, and spreadeth them out as
a tent to dwell in. . . . To whom then will ye
liken me, or shall I be equal? saith the Holy
One. Lift up your eyes on high, and behold
who hath created these things, that bringeth
out their host by number: he calleth them
all by names by the greatness of his might,

for that he is strong in power; not one faileth. (40:22, 25-26)

Now this passage is probably the most daring flight of imagination ever made by the human mind. We have here in Isaiah that which is vaster and more awesome than anything that ever came out of the mind of Shakespeare. It is the thought of the great God, the Shepherd of the universe, moving through His universe, with its billions and trillions of light years, with its worlds so big that our whole solar system would look like a grain of sand by comparison. And God stands out yonder and calls all of these millions of worlds as His sheep; He calls them all by name and leads them out across the vast sky.

I'd say this is the highest thought I know of, in the Bible or out. And God does this "by the greatness of his might, for that he is strong in power; not one faileth" (40:26). Just as a shepherd keeps all of his sheep and not one is lost, so God keeps all of His universe. Men point their tiny little glasses at the stars and talk learnedly, but they've just been counting God's sheep, nothing more. God is running His universe.

And then in the Psalms we read,

Bless the LORD, O my soul. O LORD my God, thou art very great; thou art clothed with honour and majesty. Who coverest thyself with light as with a garment: who stretchest out the heavens like a curtain: who layeth the beams of his chambers in the waters: who maketh the clouds his chariot: who walketh upon the wings of the wind. (104:1-3)

There we have the greatness, the immensity, the imminence of God, set over against the vastness and the littleness of the world. For Julian said, "I saw all of this vastness reduced, and I saw how big it actually was, set over against God Almighty. 'Twas the size of a hazelnut." Then she said, "I marveled at one thing"—and I've thought of this myself—"I marveled at what could hold it together."

God Holds What He Loves

Did you ever wonder about what held things together? Did you ever wonder why things didn't fall apart? I have! I've wondered how things didn't tear loose at the seams. "I marveled," she said, "how it might last." Since distance is all involved, since matter depends on God's word and since life is a ray from God's heart, then there isn't too much to worry about! But she said, "How can all this last, how can this hold together?" Then she said, "It came to me. I saw that all things have their being in the love of God and that God made them and God loves them and God keeps them."

That's why you don't fall apart—because God made you, God loves you and God keeps you. What God made, God loves, because it's inconceivable that God should make anything that He didn't love.

A fellow recently brought me a painting that he'd been working on quite a while, and showed it to me to see if I liked it. It's inconceivable that he didn't like his own picture. I liked it too, but it was because *he* liked it that he showed it to me. We like that which we make. And God loves that which He made. And because He made it, He loves it, and because He loves it, He keeps it.

People aren't going to lose anything they love if they can help it. A mother may lose her baby by death, but she won't do it if she can help it. A man may lose a property or his car or his job, but he won't if he can help it. And so God Almighty is in a position never to lose anything, because He's able not to lose it. He keeps it because He loves it and He loves it because He made it—or did He make it because He loves it?—I don't know.

I heard an Episcopalian rector preach a sermon on immortality. He gave one of the finest arguments for immortality that I've ever heard. "The Bible says that Abraham was a friend of God," said the rector. "Now, how would it be that a man should ever give up his friends? If a man is your friend, you wouldn't lose him if you could help it. And if he died you'd bring him back if you could. You would keep your friend if he was your friend.

"Well, God Almighty is able to keep His friend. So that's why we know that Abraham will rise again from the dead, because he is God's friend and God isn't going to allow His friend to lie around and rot forever. He's going to bring him out of the grave again. And that's why I believe in immortality. I believe that God made us and God loves what He made and is keeping what He loves."

So all things have their being in God. I want you to think of God the Maker—God the Father Almighty, Maker of heaven and earth. I want you to think of God the Lover—"God so loved the world, that he gave his only begotten Son" (John 3:16). And I want you to think of God the Keeper, if you're a real Christian. If you're not a real Christian, if you've not been born anew and washed in the blood of the Lamb, this doesn't apply to you, and there isn't any use in my trying to make it apply. But if you're a true Christian this applies to you.

Why Are We Not Happy?

As Lady Julian thought about this she said, "If this is all true, then why be we not all of great ease of heart and soul? Why aren't Christians the happiest, the most easeful people in all the wide world?" Then she answered her own question: "Because we seek to have our rest in things that are so little. This hazelnut into which is condensed all that is—we try to find our pleasure in those little things."

What is it that makes you happy? What cheers you up and gives your morale a lift? Is it your job? Is it the fact that you have good clothes? Is it that you've married well or have a fine position? Just what is it that brings you joy?

That's our trouble. We know that God is so vast

that in comparison everything is just the size of a hazelnut. And yet we're not a happy people because we've got our minds set on things. We multiply things, and we increase things and we perfect things. We beautify things and put our confidence in things *and* God. We have our job and God; we have our husband and God; we have our strong body and God; we have our good job and God; we have our home and God. We have our ambition for the future and God, and so we put God as a plus sign after something else.

All the great souls of the world from David and Paul and Augustine and all the rest down through this present hour—every responsible writer who has ever been illuminated from the Scriptures by the Holy Spirit has said the same thing. And whether he came from one school of Christian thought or another, as long as he was orthodox and spiritual he said the same thing: Our problem is that we are putting our confidence in things and not in God. And Julian said, "God showed me that all things are only the size of the hazelnut. Why therefore should I put my confidence in things so little that God has to hold it together? Why should I trust things?"

We multiply, we increase, and still we're anxious and unsatisfied. Why? Because all that is beneath God will not satisfy us. God made you in His image and you're stuck with it. God did not make the chimpanzee in His image. He did not make the horse, that symphony in motion, in His image. God did not make that beautiful bird that the poet says "sings darkling . . . his nocturnal note" in His image. God made him beautiful, but He didn't make him in His image. God made only you in His image and you're stuck with it, sinner and Christian both. You're made in the image of God, and nothing short of God will satisfy you. And even if you happen to be one of those "nickle-in-the-slot, get saved, escape hell and take heaven" Christians (that poor little kindergarten view of heaven), remember one thing—even you will find over the years that you are not content with "things plus God." You'll have to have God minus all things.

You may ask me, "Don't *you* have things?" Sure I do. God knows that I don't have much, only a lot of books. I have a wife and some children and grandchildren and friends—I have all that.

But as soon as I set my hopes and comforts upon things and people I'll lose something out of my heart. It dare not be things and God, it dare not be people and God: it must be God and nothing else. Then whatever else God gives us, we can hold at arm's length and hold it dear for Jesus' sake. And we can love it for His sake, *but it is not necessary to our happiness.* If there's anything necessary to your eternal happiness but God, you're not yet the kind of Christian that you ought to be. For only God is the true rest.

God takes great pleasure in having a helpless soul come to Him simply and plainly and intimately. He takes pleasure in having us come to Him. This kind of Christianity doesn't draw big crowds. It draws only those who have their hearts set on God, who want God more than they want anything else in the world. These people want the spiritual experience that comes from knowing God for Himself. They could have everything stripped away from them and still have God. These people are not vastly numerous in any given locality. This kind of Christianity doesn't draw big crowds, but it is likely to draw the hungriest ones, the thirstiest ones and some of the best ones. And so God takes great pleasure in having helpless people come to Him, simply and plainly and intimately. He wants us to come without all that great overloading of theology. He wants us to come as simply and as plainly as a little child. And if the Holy Spirit touches you, you'll come like that.

God's Enthusiasm

As I said in the last chapter, God is boundlessly enthusiastic. I'm glad somebody is, because I don't find very many Christians who are. If they are, they're not enthusiastic about the things that matter. If they're going to a movie, they can get all steamed up about that. If they're going on a moonlight cruise, they get all worked up over that. But if you just say, "Look, look, behold God, behold God!" you can't get much enthusiasm.

God is enthusiastic. He's enthusiastic for Himself in the Persons in the Godhead. The Persons of the Godhead are infinitely delighted with each other. The Father is infinitely delighted with the

Son, and the Son is infinitely delighted with the other two Persons of the Godhead. He is delighted with His whole creation, and especially with men made in His image. Unbelief comes and throws a cloud over us and shuts out the light of God, and we don't believe that God is delighted, infinitely delighted with us.

And here's a little prayer that was made by Lady Julian:

> O God, of Thy goodness give me Thyself, for Thou art enough for me, and I may ask nothing that is less and find any full honors to Thee. God give me Thyself!

We make out that a revival is everybody running around falling on everybody else's neck and saying, "Forgive me for thinking a bad thought about you. Forgive me for that nickel that I forgot to pay back." Or we say a revival consists of people getting very loud and noisy. Well, that might happen in a revival, but the only kind of revival that would be here when the worlds are on fire is the revival that begins by saying, "Oh God, give me Thyself! For nothing less than Thee will do."

Hunger for God

"Anything less than God," Julian said, "ever me wanteth." I like that little expression. Translated into modern English it means, "It won't be enough." Julian said in effect, "Oh God, if I have

all this hazelnut—everything from the proton to
the remotest heavenly body, up and down the
scale all the beautiful things of earth, the sky and
sea, the diamonds of the mines, the timber of the
forest, the charm of the landscape and the riches
of the cities—if I have it all and have not Thee,
ever me wanteth." It won't be enough.

The problem with the world today is that everybody is saying "ever me wanteth" and doesn't
know it. There's a little shrine inside you, a shrine
so far in that nobody can know it but you. There
is an innermost part, a deep, deep shrine, "a garden eastward in Eden" (Genesis 2:8). It lies in
that great soul of yours—that soul that is bigger
than the starry universe. There's a shrine there, a
garden and a throne. And no matter what, you'll
get a cry from that shrine: *Ever me wanteth. Oh
God, I'm still hungry, I'm still hungry!*

Who commits suicide? Not the poor—the rich.
Not the simple unknown fellow on the street—it's
the movie actors and politicians and people who
are widely known. As the song says it, "Take the
world but give me Jesus." We can have all the
world and have not Jesus, and there will be a cry
from deep within, "Ever me wanteth."

This is the greatest calamity for a human soul:
to be made in the image of God, with a spirit so
big that it can contain the universe, and yet cry for
more. Imagine a soul bigger than the heavens and
the heaven of heavens yet empty of God. Imagine
going through eternity crying, "Ever me wanteth,
O God"—forever and ever! "O God, I'm hungry

and I can't eat; I'm thirsty and I can't drink. Send Lazarus, that he may dip the tip of his finger in water, and cool my tongue; for I am tormented in this flame!" (see Luke 16:24).

I wonder if the flames of hell aren't kindled from deep in that shrine where, dry and cracked and parched, the soul of man cries, "O God, *ever me wanteth*. I've had everything: religion, position, money, a spouse and children, clothes, a good home; but it's a little hazelnut—it's nothing. O God, I've missed that which I wanted the most!"

Down at the bottom, that's the problem. That's the problem in Russia, in Washington, everywhere—ever, ever they want, though they have everything. You know the old story of Alexander, who conquered the world and wept because there was no more world to conquer. Man has gone to the North Pole and to the South Pole and now turns his greedy eyes on the moon and the planets. They have and get, they get and have.

The richest nation in the world is America. We think we're in a recession, but still cars are coming out longer and bigger and looking more like juke boxes than ever. And there's more money in more bank accounts. They may make deductions from your paycheck, but after they've taken out everything you can think of, still the average fellow has more money than he used to.

Back when I was a young fellow, a man used to raise ten kids on a dollar a day and do a good job. Now we've got everything, absolutely everything.

And yet what country in the world is the most troubled, has more breakdowns, more insanity, more murders, more triangles, more mental hospitals, more psychiatrists and couches?

God Must Be First

It's rather a cynical thought, an ironic thought, that the richest nation in the world manages to have the most divorces, the most suicides and the most juvenile delinquency. It proves again that no matter how much you give a man, if he misses God he cries, "Ever me wanteth," and goes out to do some crime. If you give him everything and then add God to it, you have wronged him, and he has wronged his own soul. For God wants to be first and wants to be all.

Money won't do it. If you take the kingdom of God and His righteousness, God will add money to you—as much as you need. If you take the kingdom of God and His righteousness, God may send your way learning and art and music and other legitimate earthly loves. God may send it all to you and let you have it. But it is always with the understanding that He can take it away again and you won't grumble. You still have God, and God is all.

Isaiah wrote: "Thy sun shall no more go down; neither shall thy moon withdraw itself: for the LORD shall be thine everlasting light, and the days of thy mourning shall be ended" (60:20). The silk weaver of Germany, Gerhard Tersteegen, wrote a kind of wild paraphrase on this:

O Fast and Gone,
How great is God,
How small am I,
A mote in the illimitable sky,
And lets the glory deep and wide and high
Of heaven's unclouded sun,
Ne'er to forget myself forevermore,
Lost, swallowed up in love's immensity.
The sea that knows no sounding and no
          shore,
God only there, not I,
Nor nearer than I am to myself can be
Art Thou to me.
So have I lost myself in finding Thee.
The boundless heaven of Thine eternal love
Around me and beneath me and above
In glory of that golden day,
The former things are passed away,
Aye, passed away.

We've almost lost our ability to kneel barefoot before such a burning bush as this. When the Church has restored to her again the kind of spirit that can understand what Isaiah meant and Tersteegen meant when he paraphrased Isaiah, then we will have revival—the kind of revival the Quakers and the Methodists had, and the kind they had at Pentecost.

So have I lost myself in finding Thee,
Have lost myself forever, O Thou Son,
The boundless heaven of Thine eternal love
Around me and beneath me and above.

This is God!

Now remember the text again: "Hid with Christ in God" (Colossians 3:3). If you gain the whole world and find not God in your own soul, what have you got? It's worth nothing to you. Let's search; let's pray; let's get still; let's get quiet. Let's learn the wonder of silence. Let's learn the beauty, the secret of seeking after God. With our Bible open before us and our knees bent, all alone in humility and penitence, let us cry, "Only God, only God and God alone! Take the world but give me Jesus!" Will you do that? We need it in the Church. We all need it. May God grant it in Jesus Christ our Lord.

Now, Father, wilt Thou bless all who receive this message? Wilt Thou grant, we pray, that we may forget the things that are behind and press forward toward the things that are ahead? Wilt Thou grant that we may see all that is as only the size of a hazelnut and ourselves in God as vast, so vast that we encompass the worlds and are utterly empty without Thee? Fill us, O God, fill us with Thyself, for without Thee ever we will be wanting. Fill us with Thyself for Jesus Christ's sake. Amen.

Chapter 3

God's Goodness

Thou art good, and doest good. (Psalm 119:68)

I will mention the lovingkindnesses of the LORD, and the praises of the LORD, according to all that the LORD hath bestowed on us, and the great goodness toward the house of Israel, which he hath bestowed on them according to his mercies, and according to the multitude of his lovingkindnesses. (Isaiah 63:7)

How precious also are thy thoughts unto me, O God! how great is the sum of them! (Psalm 139:17)

For the LORD will again rejoice over thee for good. (Deuteronomy 30:9)

How excellent is thy lovingkindness, O God! therefore the children of men put their trust under the shadow of thy wings. (Psalm 36:7)

O taste and see that the LORD is good. (Psalm 34:8)

If ye then, being evil, know how to give good
gifts unto your children, how much more shall
your Father which is in heaven give good
things to them that ask him? (Matthew 7:11)

I have for over thirty years spoken about God's goodness. It is most important that we know about God's goodness and know what kind of God He is. What is God like? It is a question that must be answered if we're going to be any kind of Christians at all. Don't take that for granted and say, "I already know."

There are those that say religion is something grafted onto man that is the result of man's weakness or superstition. However, history shows that no tribe or nation has ever risen morally above its religion. If it had a debased religion it had a debased people, and if the people were not debased, the religion, though neither Christianity nor Judaism, nevertheless was relatively high in the scale of nonrevealed religions. And remember that no religion has ever risen above its conception of God. If the heathen believe that God is tricky, sulky, nasty and deceitful, their religion will build itself around that concept. And they will try to be sneaky with their god and act the way their god acts.

If they believe, on the other hand, that God is one God, that He is a high and true and noble God, then even though they are not redeemed, their religion will tend to follow their concept of God upward, even though it is a pagan religion and does not carry redemption.

Christianity at any given time is strong or weak depending upon her concept of God. And I insist upon this and I have said it many times, that the basic trouble with the Church today is her unworthy conception of God. I talk with learned and godly people all over the country, and they're all saying the same thing.

Unbelievers say, "Take your cowboy god and go home," and we get angry and say, "They're vile heathen." No, they're not vile heathen—or at least that's not why they say that. They can't respect our "cowboy god." And since evangelicalism has gone overboard to "cowboy religion," its conception of God is unworthy of Him. Our religion is little because our god is little. Our religion is weak because our god is weak. Our religion is ignoble because the god we serve is ignoble. We do not see God as He is.

The psalmist said, "O magnify the LORD with me" (34:3). "Magnify" may mean one of two things: "make it look bigger than it is," or "see it as big as it is." The latter is what "magnify" means as the psalmist used it.

If you want to examine a very small amount of matter, you put it under a microscope and magnify it to make it look bigger than it is. But it is impossible to make God look bigger than He is. When we say "magnify the Lord," we mean try to see God somewhere near as big as He is. This is what I want to do. This is what, by His help, I have dedicated myself to do.

A local church will only be as great as its conception of God. An individual Christian will be a success or a failure depending upon what he or she thinks of God. It is critically important that we have a knowledge of the Holy One, that we know what God is like. Of course we can know from the Scriptures—that's where we go to get our information. We can know some of it from nature too: "The heavens declare the glory of God; and the firmament showeth his handiwork" (Psalm 19:1). But while the pen of nature writes without too much clarity, the Word of God is very, very clear.

It is very important that we know that God is good. We read that God is good and doeth good and that His lovingkindness is over all His works, and all of those passages of Scripture quoted above. Take a concordance and look up the word "good" or the word "lovingkindness" and see how much the Bible, both the Old and New Testaments, has to say about God being kindhearted.

What "Good" Means

God is kindhearted, gracious, good-natured and benevolent in intention. And let us remember that God is cordial. We only think we believe, really. We are believers in a sense, and I trust that we believe sufficiently to be saved and justified before His grace. But we don't believe as intensely and as intimately as we should. If we did, we would believe that God is a cordial God, that He is gracious and that His intentions are kind and benevolent. We would believe that God never thinks any bad thoughts about anybody,

and He never had any bad thoughts about anybody.

Now all this that I have said means that God is
good. All this He is infinitely. Why do I say that?
Because infinitude is an attribute of God. And it is
impossible for God to be anything and not be
completely, infinitely what He is. It is possible for
the sun to be bright, but not infinitely bright because it doesn't have all the light there is. It is
possible for a mountain to be large but not infinitely large. It is possible for an angel to be good,
but not infinitely good. Only God can claim infinitude. When I say that God is good, that God has
a kind heart, I mean that He has a heart infinitely
kind and that there is no boundary to it. When I
say that God is good-natured, good and kindly of
nature, I mean that He is infinitely so.

God is not only infinitely good, He is perfectly
good. God is never *partway* anything! When I say
that God is kindhearted, I mean that He is perfectly so. I do not mean that there are ever times
when God isn't feeling good and isn't kind.

There are never any times when God won't be
cordial. Even the best Christian doesn't always
feel cordial. Sometimes he didn't sleep well, and
though he's not mad and he's living like a Christian, he doesn't feel like talking in the mornings.
He doesn't feel cordial; he's not overflowing; he's
not enthusiastic. But there's never a time when
God isn't. Because what God is, He is perfectly.

I joyously announce to you that what God is, He
is immutably. God never changes. What God was,

God is. What God is and was, God will be. There
will never be any change in God. Don't call me a
heretic; check on me. Go to the Word and see if it's
right. If you'll be a good Berean and go to the Scriptures to see if these things are true (see Acts
17:10-11), then that's all I ask.

Remember that God is enthusiastic about His
works. God is not an absentee engineer running
His world by remote control. The Scripture says
that He is "upholding all things by the word of his
power" (Hebrews 1:3). The presence of the invisible Word in the universe makes things run. God
is the perfect creator and He runs everything by
being present in His works. That's all through the
prophets, the Psalms and the book of Job—all
through the Old Testament.

When we hit the age of science we forgot that;
we have "laws" now. The Bible knew nothing
about "the laws of nature." The Bible knew only
that God was there. If it rained, it was God water-
ing His hills from His chambers. If there was
lightning, it was God, and if there was thunder, it
was the "voice of the LORD" that "maketh the
hinds to calve" (Psalm 29:9).

The writers of Scripture were acutely
God-conscious, and they were never lonely because
God was there. "Surely the LORD is in this place; and
I knew it not," said Jacob (Genesis 28:16). This idea
that God is an absentee engineer running His universe
by remote control is all wrong. He is present in per-
petual and continuous eagerness, with all the fervor of
rapturous love pressing His holy designs. If you don't

feel that way about it, it's unbelief that makes you feel
otherwise; it's preoccupation with this world. If you
would believe God you would know this to be true.

The goodness of God means He cannot feel indifferent about anything. People are indifferent,
but not God. God either loves with a boundless
unremitting energy or He hates with consuming
fire. It was said about the second Person of the
Trinity, "Thou hast loved righteousness, and
hated iniquity; therefore God, even thy God, hath
anointed thee with the oil of gladness above thy
fellows" (Hebrews 1:9). The same Lord Jesus that
loved with boundless consuming love also hated
with terrible consuming fire and will continue to
do so while the ages roll. The goodness of God requires that God cannot love sin.

Our Reason for Living

The goodness of God is the only valid reason
for existence, the only reason underlying all
things. Do you imagine that you deserve to be
born, that you deserve to be alive? The unbeliev-
ing poet Omar Khayyám said,

Into this universe and why
not knowing nor whence
like water willy-nilly flowing
and out of it like wind along the waste,
whither I know not,
willy-nilly blowing.

And then He charged God with it all and said, "For all that I've done that's wrong, O God, forgive and take my forgiveness." He thought God owed him something. But remember that you can answer every question with this expression: "God of His goodness willed it. God out of His kindness willed it."

Why were we created? Was it that we *deserved* to be created? How can nothing deserve something? There was a time when there was no human race. How therefore could a human race that hadn't existed deserve something? How could a man that wasn't yet created earn anything or pile up any merit? It couldn't be so. God out of His goodness created us. Why were we not destroyed when we sinned? The only answer is that God of His goodness spared us. The cordial, kind-intentioned God spared us.

Why would God the Eternal Son bleed for us? The answer is, out of His goodness and lovingkindness. "Therefore the children of men put their trust under the shadow of thy wings" (Psalm 36:7). Why would God forgive me when I've sinned and then forgive me again and again? Because God out of His goodness acts according to that goodness and does what His loving heart dictates that He do.

Why does God answer prayer? Let's not imagine that it's because somebody was good. We Protestants think we don't believe in saints, but we do. We canonize them: we have Saint George Mueller, Saint C.H. Spurgeon, Saint D.L. Moody and Saint A.B. Simpson. We get the idea that God answered prayer for them because they were really good. They would deny that fervently if they were here.

Nobody ever got anything from God on the grounds that he deserved it. Having fallen, man deserves only punishment and death. So if God answers prayer it's because God is good. From His goodness, His lovingkindness, His good-natured benevolence, God does it! That's the source of everything.

These are the only grounds upon which anybody has ever been saved since the beginning of the world. There is an idea abroad that in the Old Testament men were saved by law and that in the New Testament we are saved by grace. The second is right, but the first is wrong. Nobody has ever been saved, from the day that Abel offered his bloody lamb on a homemade altar, down to the latest convert made today, except out of the goodness of God. Because of God's grace, His mercy, His lovingkindness, His goodness and graciousness, His cordiality and approachability, He kindly saved people. We've taken the word "grace" and made a technical term out of it.

The people in the Old Testament were not saved by keeping anything, because we deserved hell, and if God had acted according to justice alone, He simply would have pulled the stopper out and flushed us all down to hell and been done with it. But God out of His lovingkindness graciously forgave those who would come according to the conditions God laid down. Everybody is saved by grace. Abel was saved by grace. Noah was saved by grace—"Noah found grace in the eyes of the LORD" (Genesis 6:8). So was Moses and all the rest down to the coming of Jesus and His dying on the cross. All were saved by grace out of the goodness of God. And everybody's been saved by grace out of the goodness of God ever since.

Goodness and Severity

But let's not drown in all the syrup. God is not only good; God is severe. Romans 11:22 tells us about the severity of God: "Behold therefore the goodness and severity of God." And it says that because Israel turned away from God, God was severe with Israel and temporarily broke her off from the good olive tree and grafted in the Gentiles instead. And so behold the goodness and severity of God.

God is good toward all who accept His goodness. And for those who reject His goodness, there's nothing that even the Almighty God can do if He's going to allow man his free will—and I believe in free will. Free will was given as a gift of God—He's given us a little provisional sovereignty out of His absolute sovereignty. He has said, "I'll allow you, within a little framework, to be your own boss and to choose to go to heaven or to hell." If a man will not take God's goodness, then he must have God's severity toward all who continue in moral revolt against the throne of God and in rebellion against the virtuous laws of God.

There is nothing God can do and so His justice
disposes of all such.

But what about those who have surrendered to
His love? God, being holy as well as good, righteous as well as kindly, and we being the sinners
we are, are we not of necessity lost? Must we not
perish? Is it not moral logic that we should perish?

Let me quote from the book by Lady Julian:
"God of His goodness has ordained means to help
us, full, fair and many; the chief being that which
He took upon Him, the nature of man." In coming
to earth as a man, God came where we were, and
by coming where we were He understands us by
sympathy and empathy.

Sympathy is a good old-fashioned country
word: -*pathy* has the same root as *pathos,* which
means "feeling or suffering often"; *sym-* means
"together," such as in the word *symphony* (a
group of musicians playing *together* in harmony).
Sympathy, then, is God feeling and suffering
along with us. Empathy, of course, is a bit different. It means the ability to project yourself into
somebody else and feel as he feels. It is a wonderful theme, and every old grandmother on any old
farm in Tennessee knows what empathy means.
But it took a good scientist to give it a name.

Let me read it for you from the Bible—in biblical language instead of in the language of psychol-
ogy:

> Wherefore in all things it behoved him
> [that is, when He took on Him the seed of

Abraham] to be made like unto his brethren, that he might be a merciful and faithful high priest in things pertaining to God, to make reconciliation for the sins of the people. For in that he himself hath suffered being tempted, he is able to succour them that are tempted. (Hebrews 2:17-18)

We have not an high priest which cannot be touched with the feeling of our infirmities; but was in all points tempted like as we are, yet without sin. Let us therefore come boldly unto the throne of grace, that we may obtain mercy, and find grace to help in time of need. (4:15-16)

These are passages full of empathy. Not only does He feel along with us in our wretchedness, but He is also able to project Himself into us, so He knows how we feel and can feel with us. That is good theology.

Now God of His goodness has ordained means, "full, fair and many." And it was all out of God's goodness. We say sometimes, "The justice of God requires Him to do so and so." Never use that language—even if you hear *me* using it! There is never anything that *requires* God to do anything. God does what He does because of what He is, and there is not something standing outside of Him requiring Him to do something. He does what He does out of His own heart. All the attributes of God are simply facets of one God in three Persons.

What are these "full, fair and many" means God has made for His people? They are the precious amends that He's made for man's sins, "turning all our blame into endless worship."

We Can Boldly Approach Him

Sometimes I say things to God in prayer which are terribly bold, almost arrogant, and I've never been rebuked by God yet. They said about Luther (I'm certainly not drawing any comparison; I'd have been glad to clean his shoes and put them at his bedroom door!) that when they heard him pray it was an experience in theology. When he began to pray, he prayed with such self-abnegation, such humility, such repentance that you pitied him. But as he prayed on, he prayed with such boldness that you feared for him.

Sometimes in my private prayers I've gone to God with thoughts that I hesitate to mention, but I'm going to mention this one. Only last Friday I said to God in prayer: "I'm glad I sinned, God; I'm glad I sinned, for Thou didst come to save sinners" (see 1 Timothy 1:15).

I'm not a good man; I'm a—well, you'd have to use slang to describe me! By nature I come that way. And when I saw it in my boys, I didn't blame them. I paddled them, but I didn't blame them. I can't go to God and say, "God, I didn't do what that fellow did." I've done everything—either in actuality or in thought—that could be done. The devil himself couldn't have thought of anything that I haven't thought of in my lifetime. So I was praying to God about it and I said, "O God, these good men"—and I began naming men who, compared with me, are good men—"they can't love You as much as I do, for he who is forgiven much loves much" (see Luke 7:47).

If a doctor saves a man who has only a runny nose, he wouldn't write a book about it. He didn't do much. The fellow would get well anyhow. But the doctor who takes a man with a brain tumor, puts him asleep and, with great care, prayer and skill, brings that man back to life—he has done something.

He "saved a wretch like me." He "turned all our blame into endless worship." I believe the Bible teaches—our Lord hinted at it and Paul developed it further—that the day will come when they will gather around us from everywhere, and say, "Behold the marvels of God." You read in the book of Acts (4:14) of seeing the man that was healed standing among them, and they could say nothing. And seeing that wicked sinner standing there, we can only say, "Worthy is the Lamb that was slain" (Revelation 5:12). And worthy is the goodness of God that out of His infinite kindness, His unchanging, perfect lovingkindness, He made amends for us, "full, fair and many," turning all our sin into endless worship.

God's Kindness

Jesus is God. And Jesus is the kindest man ever to live on this earth. His kindness is something we must have. It must be a reflection, a lingering flavor, like an old vase that once held beautiful flowers. Though the vase is broken, the scent of the roses hangs round the vase. So mankind, fallen like a broken vase, dashed to the pavement and splintered into a million pieces, yet has something we call kindness.

I suppose one of the kindest men in America was Lincoln. When Lincoln visited the hospital there lay a young Northern officer so badly wounded that it was obvious that he was going to die. The nurses whispered, "Mr. President, he can't make it." And the great big, tall, homely president went into a hospital ward and walked about among the men. And then he went over to this dying young officer and stooped down, kissed his forehead and said, "Lieutenant, you've got to get well for me." And the nurses around said they heard a whispered word, "Mr. President, I'll do it." And he did!

Another time they went into his office where he sat gazing out the window over the grassy sward below, and said, "Mr. President, you seem very serious today."

"Yes," he said, "today is `butcher day.' They're going to shoot a lot of boys today in the army for retreating under fire or doing something else in wartime. I don't blame those boys; they weren't cowards. Their legs did it." Along with his tears he said, "I'm going over the list, and I'm going to save every one that I can."

That's why we love Lincoln, not just because he freed the slaves or saved the Union, but because he had a big heart. But even he had a limit. It is said that somebody once came onto the White House lawn and Lincoln's wife Mary was running and screaming. The great, tall president was following behind her with a paddle.

"What's going on here?" the person asked.

He said, "She won't obey."

He could get mad, you see. And he could act unkind, but not Jesus. The kindest man ever to draw human breath is Jesus.

A group of literary men was talking about pathos in literature. They were discussing books that moved you to tears. Matthew Arnold said of Burns that his poetry was so poignantly beautiful, piercingly pathetic, that it was hard sometimes to read because it wounds you so deeply. Somebody asked Mr. Dickens what literature he thought had the most pathos. "Oh," he said, "there is no question—the story of the Prodigal Son. There is nothing like it in all literature."

Who wrote that story? God. Who spoke it? The kindest man in all the world. When I'm reading through the Scriptures and I come to that passage, "A certain man had two sons" (Luke 15:11), instinctively I bow my head. Something in me wants to go down in obeisance before the heart that could think up that story.

God is not revolted by our wretchedness. He has no despite of anything that He has made, nor does He disdain the service in the simplest office that to our body belongeth. The Lord will be your Nurse, your Caretaker, your Helper, and He's not

revolted by anything about you. He wills that you
joy along with Him. The everlasting marvel and
the high, overpassing love of God, the irresistable
love of God, out of His goodness sees us perfect
even though we are not perfect. And He wants us
to be glad in Him.

God Wants to Please Us

He takes no pleasure in human tears. He came
and wept that He might stop up forever the fountain of human tears. He came and bereaved His
mother that He might heal all bereavement. He
came and lost everything that He might heal the
wounds that we have from losing things. And He
wants us to take pleasure in Him. Let us put away
our doubts and trust Him.

God wants to please you. He is pleased when
you are His child, when you're surrendered, when
your will is His will and His will is yours, when
you are not in rebellion and not seeking your own
will. God loves to please His people.

Did you ever see a father bringing gifts to his
children? Did you ever see a lover bringing gifts
to his bride? He wants to please the people He
loves, and the people that love Him. The idea
that God must always make you miserable is not
a biblical idea at all. Jesus Christ knew God and
He suffered from the irritations and persecutions
of the world, the bitterness of their polluted
hearts. They made it hard for Him. But He was
pleased with God and God was pleased with
Him. "This is my beloved Son, in whom I am

well pleased" (Matthew 3:17). "Well done, thou good and faithful servant" (Matthew 25:21). God can say that now to His people.

God isn't pleased by your being miserable. He will make you miserable if you won't obey, but if you're surrendered and obedient, the goodness of God has so wrought through Jesus Christ that now He wants to please you. And He wants to answer your prayers so you will be happy in Him. He wants to do that. Let's put away all doubts and trust Him.

Gerhard Tersteegen wrote a song.

> Midst the darkness storm and sorrow,
> One bright gleam I see.
> Well I know that blest tomorrow,
> Christ will come for me.

And then he writes six stanzas and the last four lines are these:

> He and I in that bright glory,
> One deep joy shall share.
> Mine to be forever with Him,
> And His that I am there.

Did you ever stop to think that God is going to be as pleased to have you with Him in heaven as you are to be there? The goodness and mercy of God, the loving kindness of the Lord—it's wonderful! He can bring us into such a relationship with Him that He can please us without spoiling us. He pleases us, and He's pleased when we're pleased. And when we're pleased with Him, He's pleased.

One common joy we will share: "mine to be forever with Him, and His that I am there." Thank God, thank God! Let us praise the lovingkindness of God forever, for of His goodness there is no end. Amen! Amen!

Chapter 4

God's Justice

Shall not the Judge of all the earth do right? (Genesis 18:25)

For the LORD your God is God of gods, and Lord of lords, a great God, a mighty, and a terrible, which regardeth not persons, nor taketh reward. (Deuteronomy 10:17)

The judgments of the LORD are true and righteous altogether. (Psalm 19:9)

To show that the LORD is upright: he is my rock, and there is no unrighteousness in him. (Psalm 92:15)

Righteousness and judgment are the habitation of his throne. (Psalm 97:2)

Judgment also will I lay to the line, and righteousness to the plummet. (Isaiah 28:17)

And I heard the angel of the waters say, Thou art righteous, O Lord, which art, and wast, and shalt be, because thou hast judged thus. For they have shed the blood of saints

*and prophets, and thou hast given them blood
to drink; for they are worthy. And I heard another out of the altar say, Even so, Lord God
Almighty, true and righteous are thy judgments. (Revelation 16:5-7)*

If you know God, you know He is absolutely
and perfectly just. But we have to define this
term first. What do we mean by justice?

In looking this up very carefully in the Scriptures, I find that justice is indistinguishable from
righteousness in the Old Testament. It's the same
root word with variations according to the part of
speech used. It means *uprightness* or *rectitude*. To
say that God is just or that the justice of God is a
fact is to say that there is uprightness and rectitude in God. Psalm 89:14 says, "Justice and judgment are the habitation of thy throne." Psalm 97:2
says, "Righteousness and judgment are the habitation of his throne." Justice and righteousness are
indistinguishable from each other.

To say that God is just is to say that God is eq-
uitable, that He is morally equal. If you go to
Ezekiel 18:25 you will find God scolding Israel
there. He says, "Yet ye say, The way of the Lord
is not equal. Hear now, O house of Israel; Is not
my way equal? are not your ways unequal?" That
word "unequal" simply means *inequity*. Do you
know that the word *inequity* and the word *iniquity* are the same word? The iniquitous person is
not morally equal, not symmetrical morally, unequal to himself.

The word "judgment" as used in the texts above is the application of justice to a moral situation, favorable or unfavorable. When God judges a man He brings justice to that man's life. He applies justice to the moral situation which that man's life created. And if the man's ways are equal, then justice favors the man. If man's ways are unequal then, of course, God sentences the man.

Justice is not something that God has. Justice is something that God *is*. A grammarian might say it should be phrased, "*Just* is something that God is." But I say, "No, *justice* is something that God is." God is love and just as God is love, God is justice.

You sometimes hear it said, "Justice requires God to do this." I've probably used this expression myself, though it is semantically improper. The human language staggers when we try to use it to describe God. The prophets of the Old Testament and the apostles of the New put such pressure on language that words groan and squeak under the effort to tell the story. We must remember that justice is not something outside of God to which God must conform. Nothing ever requires God to do anything. If you have a god who is required to do anything, then you have a weak god who has to bow his neck to some yoke and yield himself to pressure from the outside. Then justice is bigger than God. But that is to think wrongly.

All God's reasons for doing anything lie inside of God. They do not lie outside of God to be brought to bear upon Him. They lie inside of God—that is, they are what God is. And God's reasons for doing what He does spring out of what God is. Nothing has been added to God from eternity. And nothing has been removed from God from eternity. Our God is exactly what He was before a single atom was created. He will be exactly what He is when the heavens are no more. He has never changed in any way, because He is the unchanging God.

God, being perfect, is incapable of either loss or gain. He is incapable of getting larger or being smaller. He's incapable of knowing more or knowing less. God is simply God. And God acts justly from within, not in obedience to some imaginary law; He is the Author of all laws, and acts like Himself all the time.

We've been lied to, cheated, betrayed and deceived so much by even those we look up to and respect that we have come to project our cynicism to the very throne of God. And unknown to us we have within our minds a feeling that God is like that, too. Let me tell you that God always acts like Himself. There is no archangel, no 10,000 angels with swords, no cherubim or seraphim anywhere that can persuade God to act otherwise. God always acts as becomes Him and He always will.

He had to redeem man within that mighty limitless framework. He could not change, or He would have to go from better to worse or from worse to better. And being God and being perfect

He could not go either direction. He had to remain God. So in the book of Revelation, the justice of God is sung by His holy saints.

Theologians, both Jewish and Christian, speak
of justice as one of God's attributes. God is justice, and God will always act justly—not by com-
pulsion from the outside but because that's the
way He is Himself. Justice must always prevail
because God is the sovereign God who will always prevail.

If this is true, then where do you and I come in?

There was an old theologian by the name of
Anselm who isn't read much anymore. He was
one of the great church fathers, the great theologians, the great saints, the great thinkers. He was
called a second Augustine. And Anselm asked
God the question: "How dost Thou spare the
wicked if Thou art just, supremely just?"

We don't worry about this question much, because in this day we have cheapened salvation.
We have cheapened our concept of God to a place
where we expect to stumble up to the pearly gates
and bang on the door and say, "Well, God, I'm
here!" and have God take us in. We'd better get
the old theologian's question figured out lest we
presumptuously go to the gate of heaven and be
turned away.

Old brother Anselm comforted himself with
this thought: "We see where the river flows, but
the springs whence it arises we see not." He knew
God could, but he didn't know how He could.
"How canst Thou justify a wicked man and still be

just?" he asked. To that question there are three happy answers.

1. The Unity of God

One answer is that *the being of God is unitary.* What does that mean? It means that God is not composed of parts. You are not a unitary being. You are composed of spirit, soul and body. You have memory and forgetfulness. You have attributes which were given you. Some things can be taken away from you and you still can remain. There are whole sections of your brain that can be destroyed and you can still live on. You can forget, you can learn and you can still live on—that's because you are not unitary. That is, God made you, and "made" means composed. God put you together. He put the head on top of the torso and legs under the torso and He put in your bloodstream, your blood, ventricles and auricles and veins and arteries and nerves and ligaments. We were put together like that, and you can take an amazing amount of a man away and he is still there. But you can't think of God like that, because the being of God is unitary.

The Jews always believed in the unitary God. "Hear, O Israel: The LORD our God is one LORD" (Deuteronomy 6:4). Now Israel was not only saying that there is only one God. The Jews taught the unitary being of God, and the Church teaches (so far as the Church teaches anything now—you can go to church a lifetime and not get much theology) that the being of God is unitary. "There is one LORD" doesn't mean merely that there is only one God; it means that God is one.

Do you see the distinction there? We must not think of God as composed of parts working harmoniously. We must think of God as one. Because God is one, God's attributes never quarrel with each other. Because man is not unitary but made, because he is composed, the man may be frustrated. He may have schizophrenia, and part of him may war with another part of him. His sense of justice may war with his sense of mercy. The judge sits on a bench many a time and is caught between mercy and justice and doesn't know which to exercise.

There is that famous saying of the man who, on the eve of war when he had to go out and fight for his country, said to his fiancée that he loved and planned to marry, "I could not love thee so, if I loved not duty more." There's a man caught between the love of a woman and the love of duty. That's because man is made of parts. That's why we have psychiatrists—to try to get our parts back together. They don't do it, you know, but they try; we have to give them credit for trying.

God has no parts anymore than a diamond has parts. God is all one God, and everything that God does harmonizes with everything else that God does perfectly because there are no parts to get out of joint and no attributes to face each other and fight it out. All God's attributes are one, and together.

Sometimes when I preach evangelistic sermons I fall into the same semantic error. We think of God as presiding over a court of law in which the sinner has broken the law of justice. We imagine that justice is out there somewhere, outside of God. The sinner has sinned against that external justice, and he is put in handcuffs and brought before the bar of God. Then we think that God's mercy wants to forgive the sinner, but this external justice says, "No, he has broken my laws. He must die." And so we picture dramatically God sitting tearfully on His throne passing a sentence of death upon a man that His mercy wants to pardon but can't because justice won't allow it. We might just as well be pagans and think about God the way the pagans do. That's not Christian theology—never was and never can be. It is erroneous to think this way, for we are making a man out of God.

"Thou thoughtest," says God, "that I was altogether such an one as thyself " (Psalm 50:21). Our judges sit on a bench and their hearts want to pardon, but the law won't permit them and they're caught in the middle. I've been told sometimes judges turn ashen white and clutch the bench before them when they sentence men to die. Their mercy isn't harmonizing with their sense of justice. External justice stands there as a law and says, "That man shall die," but mercy says, "Please, please spare him!"

But to think thus of God is to think wrongly of God. Everything that God is and does harmonizes with everything else that God is and does. I probably should not even use the word "harmony," for harmony requires at least two that get together and for a time become one. But there is nothing like that in God; God just is! When you pray, say, "Our Father, which art in heaven." God just is!

Therefore, the first answer to the question, "How can God, being just, yet acquit the wicked?" springs from the being of God as unitary. God's justice and God's mercy do not quarrel with each other.

2. The Passion of Christ

The second answer is from the effect of Christ's passion. The word "passion" now means "sex lust," but back in the early days it meant deep, terrible suffering. That is why they call Good Friday "Passion Tide," and we talk about "the passion of Christ." It is the suffering Jesus did as He made His priestly offering with His own blood for us.

Jesus Christ is God, and all I've said about God describes Christ. He is unitary. He has taken on Himself the nature of man, but God the Eternal Word, who was before man and who created man is a unitary being and there is no dividing of His substance. And so that Holy One suffered, and His suffering in His own blood for us was three things. It was infinite, almighty and perfect.

Infinite means without bound and without limit, shoreless, bottomless, topless forever and ever, without any possible measure or limitation. And so the suffering of Jesus and the atonement He made on that cross under that darkening sky was infinite in its power.

It was not only infinite but *almighty*. It's possible for good men to "almost" do something or to "almost" be something. That is the fix people get in because they are people. But Almighty God is never "almost" anything. God is always exactly what He is. He is the Almighty One. Isaac Watts said about His dying on the cross, "God the mighty Maker died for man the creature's sin." And when God the Almighty Maker died, all the power there is was in that atonement. You never can overstate the efficaciousness of the atonement. You never can exaggerate the power of the cross.

And God is not only infinite and almighty but *perfect*. The atonement in Jesus Christ's blood is perfect; there isn't anything that can be added to it. It is spotless, impeccable, flawless. It is perfect as God is perfect. So the question, "How dost Thou spare the wicked if Thou art just?" is answered from the effect of Christ's passion. That holy suffering there on the cross and that resurrection from the dead cancels our sins and abrogates our sentence.

Where and how did we get that sentence? We got it by the application of justice to a moral situation. No matter how nice and refined and lovely you think you are, you are a moral situation—you have been, you still are, you will be. And when God confronted you, God's justice confronted a moral situation and found you unequal, found inequity, found iniquity.

Because He found iniquity there, God sentenced you to die. Everybody has been or is under the sentence of death. I wonder how people can be so jolly under the sentence of death. "The soul that sinneth, it shall die" (Ezekiel 18:20). When justice confronts a moral situation in a man, woman, young person or anybody morally responsible, then either it justifies or condemns that person. That's how we got that sentence.

Let me point out that when God in His justice sentences the sinner to die, He does not quarrel with the mercy of God; He does not quarrel with the kindness of God; He does not quarrel with His compassion or pity, for they are all attributes of a unitary God, and they cannot quarrel with each other. All the attributes of God concur in a man's death sentence. The very angels in heaven cried out and said, "Thou art righteous, O Lord, which art, and wast, and shalt be, because thou hast judged thus. . . . Even so, Lord God Almighty, true and righteous are thy judgments" (Revelation 16:5, 7).

You'll never find in heaven a group of holy beings finding fault with the way God conducts His foreign policy. God Almighty is conducting His world, and every moral creature says, "True and righteous are thy judgments. . . . Justice and judgment are the habitation of thy throne" (Revelation 16:7, Psalm 89:14). When God sends a man to die, mercy and pity and compassion and wisdom and power concur—everything that's intelligent in God concurs in the sentence.

But oh, the mystery and wonder of the atonement! The soul that avails itself of that atonement, that throws itself out on that atonement, the moral situation has changed. God has not changed! Jesus Christ did not die to change God; Jesus Christ died to change a moral situation. When God's justice confronts an unprotected sinner that justice sentences him to die. And all of God concurs in the sentence! But when Christ, who is God, went onto the tree and died there in infinite agony, in a plethora of suffering, this great God suffered more than they suffer in hell. He suffered all that they could suffer in hell. He suffered with the agony of God, for everything that God does, He does with all that He is. When God suffered for you, my friend, God suffered to change your moral situation.

The man who throws himself on the mercy of God has had the moral situation changed. God doesn't say, "Well, we'll excuse this fellow. He's made his decision, and we'll forgive him. He's gone into the prayer room, so we'll pardon him. He's going to join the church; we'll overlook his sin." No! When God looks at an atoned-for sinner He doesn't see the same moral situation that He sees when He looks at a sinner who still loves his sin. When God looks at a sinner who still loves his sin and rejects the mystery of the atonement, justice condemns him to die. When God looks at a sinner who has accepted the blood of the everlasting covenant, justice sentences him to live. And God is just in doing both things.

When God justifies a sinner everything in God is on the sinner's side. All the attributes of God are on the sinner's side. It isn't that mercy is pleading for the sinner and justice is trying to beat him to death, as we preachers sometimes make it sound. All of God does all that God does. When God looks at a sinner and sees him there unatoned for (he won't accept the atonement; he thinks it doesn't apply to him), the moral situation is such that justice says he must die. And when God looks at the atoned-for sinner, who in faith knows he's atoned for and has accepted it, justice says he must live! The unjust sinner can no more go to heaven than the justified sinner can go to hell. Oh friends, why are we so still? Why are we so quiet? We ought to rejoice and thank God with all our might!

I say it again: Justice is on the side of the returning sinner. First John 1:9 says, "If we confess our sins, he is faithful and just to forgive us our sins, and to cleanse us from all unrighteousness." Justice is over on our side now because the mystery of the agony of God on the cross has changed our moral situation. So justice looks and sees equality, not inequity, and we are justified. That's what justification means.

Do I believe in justification by faith? Oh, my brother, do I believe in it! David believed in it and wrote it into Psalm 32. It was later quoted by one of the prophets. It was picked up by Paul and written into Galatians and Romans. It was lost for awhile and relegated to the dust bin and then brought out again to the forefront and taught by Luther and the Moravians and the Wesleys and the Presbyterians. "Justification by faith"—we stand on it today.

When we talk about justification, it isn't just a text to manipulate. We ought to see who God is and see why these things are true. We're justified by faith because the agony of God on the cross changed the moral situation. *We are that moral situation.* It didn't change God at all. The idea that the cross wiped the angry scowl off the face of God and He began grudgingly to smile is a pagan concept and not Christian.

God is one. Not only is there only one God, but that one God is unitary, one with Himself, indivisible. And the mercy of God is simply God being merciful. And the justice of God is simply God being just. And the love of God is simply God loving. And the compassion of God is simply God being compassionate. It's not something that runs out of God—*it's something God is!*

3. *The Unchanging God*

How can God be just and still justify a sinner? There is a third answer. Compassion flows from goodness, and yet goodness without justice is not goodness. You couldn't be good and not be just, and if God is good He has to be just. When God punishes the wicked, it is a just thing to do, because it is consistent with the wicked man's deserts. But when God pardons a wicked man it is a just thing to do as well, because it is consistent with God's nature. So we have God the Father, Son and Holy Ghost always acting like God. Your wife may be grouchy, your best friend may be cold, foreign wars may be going on, but God is always the same. Always God acts according to His attributes of love, justice and mercy.

Always, always, always God acts like God. Aren't you glad you aren't going to sneak into heaven through a cellar window? Aren't you glad that you're not going to get in like some preachers get academic degrees, by paying twenty-five dollars to a diploma factory?

Aren't you glad that you're not going to get into heaven by God's oversight? God is so busy with His world that you sneak in. You're there a thousand years before God sees you!

Aren't you glad that you're not going to get in just by being a member of a church? God says, "Well, that's a pretty good church. Let's let him in." And so you go in, but later on He finds your rotten spots and maybe you'll be thrown out!

There is the parable of the man who appeared without a wedding garment. And after he got in, they said, "What is he doing here?" and they threw him out—bound him hand and foot, lugged him out and threw him into outer darkness (see Matthew 22:11-13). There'll be nothing like that in God's kingdom, because God the All-Wise One knows all that can be known. He knows everybody—He knows you. And God the All-Just One will never permit the unequal man in there. "Why walk ye along on two unequal legs?" said Elijah (1

Kings 18:21, author's paraphrase). That's unequal, iniquity. And the man who is iniquitous will never get in. Never!

All of this cheap talk about St. Peter giving us an exam to see if we're all right—it's all nonsense! The Great God Almighty, always one with Himself, looks upon a moral situation and He either sees death or life. And all of God is on the side of death or life. If there is an iniquitous, unequal, unatoned, uncleansed, unprotected sinner in his sin, there's only one answer—all of God says, "Death and hell." And all of heaven can't pull that man up.

But if he beats his breast and says, "God be merciful to me a sinner" (Luke 18:13), and takes the benefits of the infinite agony of God on a cross, God looks on that moral situation and says, "Life!" And all of hell can't drag that man down. Oh, the wonder and the mystery and the glory of the being of God!

Chapter 5

God's Mercy

The LORD is merciful and gracious, slow to anger and plenteous in mercy. He will not always chide: neither will he keep his anger for ever. He hath not dealt with us after our sins; nor rewarded us according to our iniquities. For as the heaven is high above the earth, so great is his mercy toward them that fear him. As far as the east is from the west, so far hath he removed our transgressions from us. Like as a father pitieth his children, so the LORD pitieth them that fear him. For he knoweth our frame; he remembereth that we are dust. As for man, his days are as grass: as a flower of the field, so he flourisheth. For the wind passeth over it, and it is gone; and the place thereof shall know it no more. But the mercy of the LORD is from everlasting to everlasting upon them that fear him, and his righteousness unto children's children. (Psalm 103:8-17)

Blessed be God, even the Father of our Lord Jesus Christ, the Father of mercies, and the God of all comfort. (2 Corinthians 1:3)

Ye have heard of the patience of Job, and have seen the end of the Lord; that the Lord is very pitiful, and of tender mercy. (James 5:11)

The Lord is not slack concerning his promise, as some men count slackness; but is long-suffering to us-ward, not willing that any should perish, but that all should come to repentance. (2 Peter 3:9)

Mercy, then, is an attribute of God. In Exodus there is a wonderfully moving declaration that one attribute of God is mercy:

Moses rose up early in the morning, and went up unto mount Sinai. . . . And the LORD descended in the cloud, and stood with him there, and proclaimed the name of the LORD. And the LORD passed by before him, and proclaimed, The LORD, The LORD God, merciful and gracious, longsuffering, and abundant in goodness and truth. Keeping mercy for thousands, forgiving iniquity and transgression and sin. (34:4-7)

And in Second Chronicles, in the temple, there is another great declaration of God's mercy:

It came even to pass, as the trumpeters and

singers were as one, to make one sound to
be heard in praising and thanking the LORD
and when they lifted up their voice with the
trumpets and cymbals and instruments of
musick, and praised the LORD, saying, For
he is good; for his mercy endureth for ever:
that then the house was filled with a cloud,
even the house of the LORD; so that the
priests could not stand to minister by reason
of the cloud: for the glory of the LORD had
filled the house of God. (5:13-14)

These two passages set forth in rather formal
style a declaration that God is merciful. As I said
about the other attributes of the Deity, mercy is
not something God *has* but something God *is*. If
mercy was something God had, conceivably God
might mislay it or use it up. It might become less
or more. But since it is something that God is,
then we must remember that it is uncreated. The
mercy of God did not come into being. The mercy
of God always was in being, for mercy is what
God is, and God is eternal. And God is infinite.

There has been a lot of careless teaching that
implies that the Old Testament is a book of severity and law, and the New Testament is a book of
tenderness and grace. But do you know that while
both the Old Testament and the New Testament
declare the mercy of God, the word *mercy* appears
in the Old Testament over four times more often
than in the New? That's a bit hard to believe, but
it's true.

This popular idea is a great error because the God of the Old Testament and the God of the New is one God. He did not change. He is the same God and, being the same God and not changing, He must therefore necessarily be the same in the Old as He is in the New. He is immutable, and because He is perfect He cannot be added to. God's mercy was just as great in the Old Testament as it was and is in the New.

Goodness is the source of mercy. I must apologize here for my necessity to use human language to speak of God. Language deals with the finite, and God is infinite. When we try to describe God or talk about God we're always breaking our own rules and falling back into the little semantic snares which we don't want to fall into but can't help. When I say that one attribute is the source of another, I'm not using correct language, but I'm putting it so you can get hold of it. If I tried to use absolutes, you'd all fall sound asleep.

God's infinite goodness is taught throughout the entire Bible. Goodness is that in God which desires the happiness of His creatures and that irresistible urge in God to bestow blessedness. The goodness of God takes pleasure in the pleasure of His people. I wish I could teach the children of God to know this. For a long time it has been drummed into us that if we are happy, God is worried about us. We believe He's never quite pleased if we are happy. But the strict, true teaching of the Word is that God takes pleasure in the pleasure of His people, provided His people take pleasure in God.

> I will mention the lovingkindnesses of the LORD, and the praises of the LORD, according to all that the LORD hath bestowed on us, and the great goodness toward the house of Israel, which he hath bestowed on them according to his mercies, and according to the multitude of his lovingkindnesses. For he said, Surely they are my people, children that will not lie: so he was their Saviour. In all their affliction he was afflicted, and the angel of his presence saved them: in his love and in his pity he redeemed them; and he bare them, and carried them all the days of old. (Isaiah 63:7-9)

God takes pleasure in the pleasure of His friends and He suffers along with these friends. He takes no pleasure in the suffering of His enemies. "As I live, saith the Lord GOD, I have no pleasure in the death of the wicked; but that the wicked turn from his way and live" (Ezekiel 33:11). God never looks down and rejoices to see somebody squirm. If God has to punish, God is not pleased with Himself for punishing. "I have no pleasure in the death of the wicked."

According to the Old Testament, mercy has certain meanings: to stoop in kindness to an inferior, to have pity upon and to be actively compassionate. It used to be a verb form of the word

compassion, but we don't use it anymore—
maybe because we don't have the concept anymore. God actively "compassionates" suffering
men—I like that wonderfully well. For God to
feel compassion at a distance is one thing, but
for God to be actively compassionate with people
is something else. Read what the Word of God
says about it:

> And the children of Israel sighed by reason
> of the bondage, and they cried, and their cry
> came up unto God by reason of the bond-
> age. And God heard their groaning, and God
> remembered his covenant with Abraham,
> with Isaac, and with Jacob. And God looked
> upon the children of Israel, and God had re-
> spect unto them. (Exodus 2:23-25)

That is at the close of the second chapter of Exodus. And the third chapter opens with the burning bush and goes on to the commissioning of
Moses to go deliver Israel from Egypt.

When God actively exercised compassion on
these people He did four things: He heard their
groanings; He remembered His covenant; He
looked upon their sufferings and pitied them; and
He immediately came down to help them. The
same thing is true in the New Testament, where it
is said of our Lord Jesus that when He saw the multitude, He "was moved with compassion toward
them, because they were as sheep not having a
shepherd" (Mark 6:34). He said to the disciples,

"Give ye them to eat" (6:37). That is being actively compassionate.

A great many people are very merciful in their beds, in their lovely living rooms, in their new cars. They have compassion (a noun), but they never "compassionate" (a verb). They read something in the newspaper about somebody suffering and say, "Aw, isn't that terrible! That poor family was burned out and they're out on the street with no place to go," and then they turn the radio on and listen to some program. They're very compassionate—for a minute and a half—but they don't "compassionate"; that is, they don't do anything about it. But God's compassion leads Him to actively "compassionate." He did it by sending Moses down to deliver the children of Israel.

One fact about the mercy of God is that *it never began to be.* I've heard of men who were hardhearted or careless, but they began to get stirred up and mercy blossomed forth. It never was so of God. God never lay in lethargy without His compassion. God's mercy is simply what God is—uncreated and eternal. It never began to be; it always was. Heaven and earth were yet unmade and the stars were yet unformed and all that space men are talking about now was only a thought in the mind of God. God was as merciful as He is now. And not only did it never begin to be, but the mercy of God also has never been any more than it is now.

Scientists tell us that there are heavenly bodies that disappeared in a grand explosion so many light-years away that it will yet be thousands of earth years before their light stops shining. The light is still coming, though the source of the light has long ceased to be. And there are stars that burn up bright and dim down low again, but the mercy of God has never been any more than it is now for the simple reason that the mercy of God is infinite, and anything that is infinite can't be less than it is, and it can't be any more than it is. It is infinite, boundless, unlimited; it has no measurements on any side. Measurements are created things, and God is uncreated.

The mercy of God has never been any more than now, and the mercy of God will never be any less than now. Don't imagine that when the day of judgment comes God will turn off His mercy as the sun goes behind a cloud or as you turn off a spigot. Don't think for a minute that the mercy of God will cease to be. The mercy of God will never be any less than it is now, because the infinite cannot cease to be infinite, and the perfect cannot admit an imperfection. And again, nothing that occurs can increase the mercy of God or diminish the mercy of God or alter the quality of the mercy of God.

For instance, the cross of Christ. When Jesus died on the cross the mercy of God did not become any greater. It could not become any greater, for it was already infinite. We get the odd notion that God is showing mercy because Jesus died. No—Jesus died because God is showing mercy. It was the mercy of God that gave us Cal-

vary, not Calvary that gave us mercy. If God had
not been merciful there would have been no incarnation, no babe in the manger, no man on a
cross and no open tomb.

God has mercy enough to enfold the whole universe in His heart, and nothing anybody ever did
could diminish the mercy of God. A man can
walk out from under and away from the mercy of
God as Israel did and as Adam and Eve did for a
time, as the nations of the world have done, and
as Sodom and Gomorrah did. We can make the
mercy of God inoperative toward us by our con-
duct, since we are free moral agents. But that
doesn't change or diminish the power of the
Word of God nor the mercy of God. And it does-
n't alter the quality of it.

The intercession of Christ at the right hand of
God does not increase the mercy of God toward His
people. If God were not already merciful, there
would be no intercession of Christ at the right hand
of God. And if God is merciful at all then He is infinitely merciful. It is impossible for the mediatorship
of Jesus at the right hand of the Father to make the
mercy of God any more than it is now.

No attribute of God is greater than any other
one. We think so. But since all of the attributes of
God are simply God, then it's impossible that anything in God can be greater than anything else in
God. That's good theology. You can't argue it
down; it's true.

And yet there are attributes of God that can be
needed more at various times. For instance, when

the Good Samaritan went along and saw the fellow who had been beaten up by robbers lying there, the most needed attribute at that moment was mercy. He needed somebody to "compassionate" him. And so the Good Samaritan got down off his beast and went over and "compassionated" him. That's what he needed at the time.

And that's why the mercy of God is so wonderful to a sinner who comes home that he wants to write about it and talk about it forever. It was what he needed so desperately at the moment. We sing, "Amazing grace, how sweet the sound," and yet the grace of God is not any greater than the justice of God or the holiness of God. But for people like you and me, it is what we need the most desperately. It isn't God who is different; it's us. You could go to heaven and say to an angel, "Isn't the mercy of God wonderful?" He'll know that it is, but he won't understand it the way we do.

Charles Finney said in his great little hymn, "These creatures round the throne, they have never, never known a sinful world like this." They cannot appreciate the love and mercy of God as we can. They talk about the holiness, the judgment and the justice of God, and they sing to Him, "righteous are thy judgments" (Revelation 16:7), because they have never known sin. Therefore they are not in need of mercy as you and I are.

God is equal to Himself always. But when you're in a jam, you need certain attributes more than others. When I'm in the doctor's office I need pity.

I want help. I can look up at the wall and see his diplomas and know that he's educated. But I just want him to be nice to me because I'm always scared when I go to a doctor. And when we come to God our need determines which of God's attributes at the moment we'll celebrate. And we'll have a thousand of them to celebrate.

The Operation of God's Mercy

The judgment of God is God's justice confronting moral inequity and iniquity. When justice sees iniquity, judgment falls. Mercy is God's goodness confronting human guilt and suffering. When the goodness of God confronts human guilt and suffering, God listens, God hears, and the bleating of the lamb comes into His ear and the moan of the babe comes into His heart, and the cry of Israel comes up to His throne. The goodness of God is confronting human suffering and guilt, and that is mercy.

All men are recipients of God's mercy. Don't think for a minute that when you repented and came back from the swine pen to the Father's house that mercy then began to operate. No, mercy had been operating all the time. Lamentations 3:22 says, "It is of the LORD's mercies that we are not consumed, because his compassions fail not." So remember that if you hadn't had the mercy of God all the time, stooping in pity, withholding judgment, you'd have perished long ago. The cruel dictator is a recipient of the mercy of God. The wicked murderer is a recipient of the mercy of God. And the blackest heart that lies in the lowest wallow in the country is a recipient of the mercy of God. That doesn't mean they'll be saved or converted and finally reach heaven. But it means that God is holding up His justice because He's having mercy. He is waiting because a Savior died. All of us are recipients of the mercy of God.

You may ask, "When I am forgiven and cleansed and delivered, isn't that the mercy of God?" Sure, that's the mercy of God to you, but all the time you were sinning against Him, He was having pity on you. "The Lord is . . . not willing that any should perish" (2 Peter 3:9). Romans 2:4 says, "Despisest thou the riches of his goodness and forbearance and longsuffering?" He is waiting. God would take this world and squeeze it in His hand as a child might squeeze a robin's egg and destroy it out of mind forever, except that He is a merciful God. He sees our tears and hears our groans in all His love and mercy. He is conscious of our suffering down here.

All men are recipients of the mercy of God, but God has postponed the execution, that is all. When the justice of God confronts human guilt then there is a sentence of death, but the mercy of God—because that also is an attribute of God, not contradicting the other but working with it—postpones the execution.

Mercy cannot cancel judgment apart from atonement. When justice sees iniquity, there must be judgment. But mercy brought Christ to the cross. I don't claim to understand that. I'm so

happy about the things I do know and so delight-
edly happy about things I don't know.

I don't know what happened there on that cross,
exactly; I know He died. God the mighty Maker
died for the sin of man, the creature. I know that
God turned His back on that holy, holy, holy Man.
I know that He gave up the ghost and died. I know
that in heaven is registered atonement for all mankind. I know that! And still I don't know why, and
I don't know what happened.

I only know that in the infinite goodness of
God and His infinite wisdom He wrought out a
plan whereby the second Person of the Trinity, incarnated as a man, could die in order that justice
might be satisfied while mercy rescued the man
for whom He died.

That's Christian theology. Whatever your de-
nomination, that's what you want to go to heaven
on. You can't go to heaven on spirituals and cho-
ruses and cheap books, but you can go to heaven
on the mercy of God in Christ. That's what the Bible teaches. Justification means that mercy and
justice have collaborated so that when God turns
and sees iniquity, and then sees the man of iniquity rushing to the cross, He no longer sees iniquity but justification. And so we're justified by
faith.

The Suffering of God

I said before that God takes pleasure in the
pleasure of His people and suffers along with His
friends. "In all their affliction he was afflicted"

(Isaiah 63:9). If you are a good tight thinker, you may ask, "How can a perfect God suffer?" Suffering means that somewhere there is a disorder. You don't suffer as long as you have psychological, mental and physical order; when you get out of order you suffer.

As long as it is declared in the Bible, you must take it by faith and say, "Father, I believe it." And then because you believe, you try to understand. And if you can understand, then thank God; your little intellect can have fun leaping about rejoicing in God.

But if you read it in the Bible and your intellect can't understand it, then there's only one thing to do, and that is to look up and say, "O Lord GOD, thou knowest" (Ezekiel 37:3). There is an awful lot we don't know. The trouble with us evangelicals is that we know too much! We're too slick; we have too many answers. I'm looking for the fellow who will say, "I don't know, but oh Lord God, Thou knowest." There's someone who is spiritually wise.

So how can God suffer? Suffering would seem to indicate some imperfection, and yet we know that God is perfect. Suffering would seem to indicate some loss or lack and yet we know that God can suffer no loss and that He cannot lack, because God is infinitely perfect in all His being. I do not know how to explain this. I only know that the Bible declares that God suffers with His children and that in all their affliction He is afflicted. In His love and in His mercy He carries them and He makes their bed in their sickness. I know this but I don't know how.

A great old theologian once said, "Don't reject a fact because you don't know a method." Don't say it isn't so because you don't know how it's so. There is much you can't explain. If you come to me and ask me the how of things, I'll ask you twenty-five questions, one after the other, about yourself—your body, your mind, your hair, your skin, your eyes, your ears. You won't be able to answer one question. Yet you use all those things even though you don't understand them. I don't know how God can suffer. That is a mystery I may never know.

A lot of hymn writers who should have been cutting the grass at the time have written songs instead. One of them says this: "I wonder why, I wonder why He loved me so. I will love and pray that I might know why He loved me so." You will never know that. There is only one answer to why God loved you: because God is love. And there is only one answer to why God has mercy on you: because God is mercy, and mercy is an attribute of the Deity. Don't ask God why, but thank Him for the vast wondrous how and fact of it.

I'm going to paraphrase a little quatrain written by Faber about how God can suffer:

How Thou canst suffer, O my God,
And be the God Thou art
Is darkness to my intellect
But sunshine to my heart.

I don't know how He does it, but I know that when I'm sick, God's sad, and I know that when I'm miserable, God suffers along with me. And I know that in all my sickness, He'll make my bed because His name is goodness and His name is mercy.

The Nearness of God's Mercy

The nearness of God's mercy is "as a father pitieth his children" (Psalm 103:13). After the first World War the United States with its big heart gave vast sums of money to the dislocated orphans of Europe, but they didn't have enough to meet the need. In one of the places where they were taking in orphans, a man came in, very thin, with large, unnaturally bright eyes, thin cheeks and thin arms, leading a little girl. She also showed signs of malnutrition—eyes too large and bright, her little abdomen distended and her thin little legs and arms too small and too thin for her age.

This man led her in and said to the person in charge, "I would like you to take in my little girl." And they asked him if she was his daughter.

"Yes," he said.

"Well," they said, "we're awfully sorry, but our rule here is that only full orphans can receive any help. If one of the parents is living then we can't take responsibility because we just don't have enough. There are too many full orphans for us to take a half orphan."

And he looked down at his little girl, and she

looked up questioningly with big, too-bright eyes, and then he turned and said, "Well, you know, I can't work. I'm sick. I've been abused. I have been in prison. I've been half starved, and now I'm old and I can't work. I can barely stagger around. But I brought her down for you to take care of her."

And they said, "We're sorry, but there's nothing we can do."

He said, "You mean that if I were dead, you'd take care of my little girl and feed her and she could live and have clothing and a home?" They said, "Yes." Then he reached down and pulled her little skinny body up to himself and hugged her hard and kissed her. Then he put her hand in the hand of the man at the desk, and said, "I'll arrange that," and walked out of the room and committed suicide.

I heard that story years ago and I haven't gotten over it yet. Still I see that picture of the man who was too sick to work but who stood in the way of his daughter's getting decent food and clothing. And he said, "I'll take care of that," and he did. That's mercy—as a father pitieth his children, so the Lord pities them that fear Him.

Jesus said, "The Son of man is delivered into the hands of men, and they shall kill him" (Mark 9:31). Peter said, "Lord: this shall not be unto thee" (Matthew 16:22). But Jesus said, in effect, "If I don't, you don't live." And so He went out not to slay Himself but to put Himself where they could slay Him. Mercy was showing compassion in the only way it could at the moment, by dying. So Christ Jesus our Lord died there on that cross, for He loved us and pitied us as a father pities his children.

Our Response to God's Mercy

We who have received mercy must show mercy. We must pray that God will help us to show mercy. We've received it; we've got to show it. This mercy can only come by atonement. Mercy can only operate toward us because of atonement. But atonement has been made.

In a hymn written around the book of Hebrews it says:

> Where high the heavenly temple stands,
> The house of God not made with hands,
> The great High Priest our nature wears,
> The Guardian of mankind appears.
>
> Though now ascended up on high
> He bends on earth a brother's eye.
> Partaker of the human name,
> He knows the frailty of our frame.
>
> Our Fellow Sufferer now retains
> A fellow feeling of our pains,
> And still remembers in the skies
> His tears, His agonies, and cries.
>
> In every pang that rends the heart
> The Man of Sorrows has a part.

He sympathizes with our grief
And to the sufferer sends relief.

With boldness therefore at the throne
Let us make all our sorrows known
And ask the aid of heavenly power
To help us in the evil hour.

How wonderful this is! Our great High Priest, who is the Guardian of man, wears our nature before the throne of God. If you went up there near the throne and God would allow you to look—though I don't know how you can look on that awesome sight—there would be creatures you couldn't identify. There would be strange creatures there before the throne having four faces and "six wings; with twain he covered his face, and with twain he covered his feet, and with twain he did fly" (Isaiah 6:2). You would see strange angels there such as Abraham saw and Jacob saw going up and down the ladder. You wouldn't be able to identify them because you've never seen an angel. I suppose there are other creatures there; I read about them in Daniel and Revelation.

But I know that as you drew near the throne, you would recognize one order of being. You would say, "Look, look, look, I recognize this! I'm familiar with this shape; this form I know! This is a man, this has two legs under him, this has two arms, this is a man!"

"The great High Priest our nature wears, and the

Guardian of mankind appears." Though you might
be very much a stranger among those strange creatures yonder, there would be one Being you would
know. You would say, "I grew up among them; I
knew them; I've seen them go down the street; I've
seen little ones and big ones and black ones and
yellow ones and red ones. I know this is a man."

And He would smile down from the throne, because "though now ascended up on high, He
bends on earth a brother's eye. Partaker of the human name, He knows the frailty of our frame."

Don't pity yourself. Don't be afraid to tell God
your troubles. He knows all about your troubles.
There is a little song that says, "Nobody knows
the trouble I've seen," but there's Somebody who
knows, all right. And our Fellow Sufferer still re-
tains a fellow feeling for our pains and still re-
members in the skies His tears, His agonies and
cries, though He's now at the right hand of the
Father Almighty, sitting crowned in glory, await-
ing, of course, that great coronation day that yet is
to come. But though He is there and though they
cry all around Him, "Worthy is the Lamb" (Revelation 5:12), He hasn't forgotten us, and He hasn't
forgotten the nails in His hands, the tears, the agonies and cries.

He knows everything about you. He knows! He
knows when the doctor hates to tell you what's
wrong with you and your friends come and try to
be unnaturally encouraging. He knows!

With boldness, therefore, at the throne
Let us make all our sorrows known
And ask the aid of heavenly power
To help us in the evil hour.

"The mercy of God is an ocean divine, a bound-less and fathomless flood." Let us plunge out into the mercy of God and come to know it. I hope you believe this, because you're going to need this mercy desperately if you don't already have it. The mercy of God in Christ Jesus—amen and amen!

Chapter 6

God's Grace

But Noah found grace in the eyes of the LORD. (Genesis 6:8)

And the LORD said unto Moses, I will do this thing also that thou hast spoken: for thou hast found grace in my sight, and I know thee by name. (Exodus 33:17)

Surely he scorneth the scorners: but he giveth grace unto the lowly. (Proverbs 3:34)

And of his fulness have all we received, and grace for grace. For the law was given by Moses, but grace and truth came by Jesus Christ. (John 1:16-17)

Being justified freely by his grace through the redemption that is in Christ Jesus. (Romans 3:24)

For if through the offence of one many be dead, much more the grace of God, and the gift by grace, which is by one man, Jesus Christ, hath abounded unto many. (Romans 5:15)

*To the praise of the glory of his grace,
wherein he hath made us accepted in the beloved. In whom we have redemption through
his blood, the forgiveness of sins, according to
the riches of his grace. (Ephesians 1:6-7)*

*But the God of all grace, who hath called us
unto his eternal glory by Christ Jesus. . . .*
(1 Peter 5:10)

As was said before, an attribute is something God *is*, not something God *has*.
Grace is therefore something God is. Its
meaning is close to, but not the same as, mercy.
Just as mercy flows out of the goodness of God, so
grace flows out of the goodness of God.

Grace Flows from God's Goodness

Mercy, however, is God's goodness confronting
human guilt, whereas grace is God's goodness
confronting human demerit. (There is a difference
between no merit and demerit. *No merit* is simply
a lack; *demerit* means that there is not only no
merit there but that there is the opposite of
merit.) When justice confronts a moral situation,
it pronounces death; there is divine disapproval to
the point of condemnation. God must stand
against the man, because the man stands with his
sin; justice must judge. Still, the goodness of God
yearns to bestow blessedness even to those who
do not deserve it, but who have a specific demerit,
and that blessedness is grace.

Grace is God's good pleasure, and it is what God

is like. I have said over and over again that one of the big problems of the Church is the loss of the proper concept of what God is like. And if we could restore that again, we could have an army of preachers going up and down the land preaching about what God is like. Pastors and teachers would begin again to tell the people what God is like. It would put strength and foundation under our faith again.

Grace is that in God which brings into favor one justly in disfavor. I'm actually staying very close to the Hebrew and Greek definitions. Grace and favor, incidentally, are often used interchangeably in the English Bible. There is four times as much said about mercy in the Old Testament as in the New. But strangely and wonderfully there is more than three times as much said about grace in the New Testament as in the Old.

"The law was given by Moses, but grace and truth came by Jesus Christ" (John 1:17). Christ is the channel through which grace flows. It is possible to misunderstand this. We have made it to mean that Moses knew only law and Christ knows only grace. This is the typical teaching of the hour, but it is not the teaching of our fathers. You'll not find it in John Bunyan or John Owen or Henry Scougal or any of the Puritans. You'll not find it even in Calvin. You'll not find it among the great revivalists and Church fathers and reformers.

To think that because the law was given by Moses, therefore Moses knew no grace, is to misread that passage. Genesis 6:8 says, "Noah found grace in the eyes of the LORD" before there was any law given. And after the law was given, after Moses had been on the mount forty days and forty nights, and God had reached down out of the fire and storm and with His finger had chiseled the Ten Commandments on the tables of stone, it says, "Thou hast found grace in my sight, and I know thee by name" (Exodus 33:17).

God did not deal with Moses on the basis of law. He dealt with Moses on the basis of grace. And Moses knew it and said, "If I have found grace in thy sight, shew me now thy way, that I may know thee, that I may find grace in thy sight" (33:13).

How could it be that God should act only in law in the Old Testament and only in grace in the New if God doesn't change? If immutability is an attribute of God, then God must always act like Himself. Grace doesn't ebb and flow like the tide; it doesn't come like the weather. God must always act like Himself—before the flood and after the flood, when the law was given and after the law was given. Grace is an attribute of God, that is, something which God is and which cannot be removed from God and yet have God remain God. There was always grace in the heart of God, and there isn't any more grace now than there ever was, and there will never be any more grace than there is now.

Grace: The Only Means of Salvation

Here are two important truths. (And I want you to take it and the next time you hear a professor or a preacher say otherwise, go to him and remind him of this.) The first truth is that no one ever was saved, no one is now saved and no one ever will be saved except by grace. Before Moses nobody was ever saved except by grace. During Moses' time nobody was ever saved except by grace. After Moses and before the cross and after the cross and since the cross and during all that dispensation, during any dispensation, anywhere, any time since Abel offered his first lamb before God on the smoking altar—nobody was ever saved in any other way than by grace.

The second truth is that grace always comes by Jesus Christ. The law was given by Moses, but grace came by Jesus Christ. This does not mean that before Jesus was born of Mary there was no grace. God dealt in grace with mankind, looking forward to the Incarnation and death of Jesus before Christ came. Now, since He's come and gone to the Father's right hand, God looks back upon the cross as we look back upon the cross. Everybody from Abel on was saved by looking forward to the cross. Grace came by Jesus Christ. And everybody that's been saved since the cross is saved by looking back at the cross.

Grace always comes by Jesus Christ. It didn't come at His birth, but it came in God's ancient plan. No grace was ever administered to anybody except by and through and in Jesus Christ. When Adam and Eve had no children God spared Adam and Eve by grace. And when they had their two boys, one offered a lamb and thus said, "I look forward to the Lamb of God." He accepted the grace of Christ Jesus thousands of years before He was born, and God gave him witness that he was justified.

The grace did not come when Christ was born in a manger. It did not come when Christ was baptized or anointed of the Spirit. It did not come when He died on a cross; it did not come when He rose from the dead. It did not come when He went to the Father's right hand. Grace came from the ancient beginnings through Jesus Christ the eternal Son and was manifest on the cross of Calvary, in fiery blood and tears and sweat and death. But it has always been operative from the beginning. If God had not operated in grace He would have swept the human race away. He would have crushed Adam and Eve under His heel in awful judgment, for they had it coming.

But because God was a God of grace, He already had an eternity planned—the plan of grace, "the Lamb slain from the foundation of the world" (Revelation 13:8). There was no embarrassment in the divine scheme; God didn't have to back up and say, "I'm sorry, but I have mixed things up here." He simply went right on.

Everybody receives in some degree God's grace: the lowest woman in the world; the most sinful, bloody man in the world; Judas; Hitler. If it hadn't been that God was gracious, they would have been cut off and slain, along with you and me and all the rest. I wonder if there's much difference in us sinners after all.

When a woman sweeps up a house, some of the dirt is black, some is gray, some is light-colored, but it is all dirt, and it all goes before the broom. And when God looks at humanity He sees some that are morally light-colored, some that are morally dark, some that are morally speckled, but it is all dirt, and it all goes before the moral broom. So the grace of God is operated toward everybody. But the saving grace of God is different. When the grace of God becomes operative through faith in Jesus Christ then there is the new birth. But the grace of God nevertheless holds back any judgment that would come until God in His kindness has given everyone a chance to repent.

Grace Is What God Is Like

Grace is God's goodness, the kindness of God's heart, the good will, the cordial benevolence. It is what God is like. God is like that all the time. You'll never run into a stratum in God that is hard. You'll always find God gracious, at all times and toward all peoples forever. You'll never run into any meanness in God, never any resentment or rancor or ill will, for there is none there. God has no ill will toward any being. God is a God of utter kindness and cordiality and good will and benevolence. And yet all of these work in perfect harmony with God's justice and God's judgment. I believe in hell and I believe in judgment. But I also believe that there are those whom God must reject because of their impenitence, yet there will be grace. God will still feel gracious toward all of His universe. He is God and He can't do anything else.

Grace is infinite, but I don't want you to strain to understand infinitude. I had the temerity to preach on infinitude a few times, and I got along all right—at least *I* got along all right. Let's try to measure it against ourselves, not against God. God never measures anything in Himself against anything else in Himself. That is, God never measures His grace against His justice or His mercy against His love. God is all one. But God measures His grace against our sin. "Grace . . . hath abounded unto many," says Romans 5:15, "according to the riches of his grace" (Ephesians 1:7). And, says Romans 5 again, "But where sin abounded, grace did much more abound" (5:20). God says "much more abound," but God has no degrees. Man has degrees.

One of the worst things you can do is to give people IQ tests. When I was in the army I had an IQ test and I rated very high, and I have had a lifetime of trying to keep from remembering that and keeping humble before God. I think how I rated up in the top four percent in all of the army, and of course, you know what that does to a person. You have to keep humbling yourself, and God has to keep chastening you to keep you down.

But there's nothing in God that can compare itself with anything else in God. What God is, God is! When Scripture says grace does "much more abound," it means not that grace does much more abound than anything else in God but much more than anything in us. No matter how much sin a man has done, literally and truly grace abounds unto that man.

Old John Bunyan wrote his life story and called it—I think it was one of the finest titles ever given to a book—*Grace Abounding Toward the Chief of Sinners*. Bunyan honestly believed that he was the man who had the least right to the grace of God. Grace abounded! For us who stand under the disapproval of God, who by sin lie under sentence of God's eternal, everlasting displeasure and banishment, grace is an incomprehensibly immense and overwhelming plenitude of kindness and goodness. If we could only remember it, we wouldn't have to be played with and entertained so much. If we could only remember the grace of God toward us who have nothing but demerit, we would be overwhelmed by this incomprehensibly immense attribute, so vast, so huge, that nobody can ever grasp it or hope to understand it.

Would God have put up with us this long if He had only a limited amount of grace? If He had only a limited amount of anything, He wouldn't be God. I shouldn't use the word "amount," because "amount" means "a measure," and you can't measure God in any direction. God dwells in no dimension and can be measured in no way. Measures belong to human beings. Measures belong to the stars.

Distance is the way heavenly bodies account for the space they occupy and their relation to other heavenly bodies. The moon is 250,000 miles away. The sun is 93 million miles away, and all that sort of thing. But God never accounts to anybody for anything He is. God's immensity, God's infinitude must mean that the grace of God must always be immeasurably full. We sing "Amazing Grace" —why, of course it's amazing! How can we comprehend the fullness of the grace of God?

How to Look at Grace

There are two ways to think about the grace of God: One is to look at yourself and see how sinful you were and say, "God's grace must be vast—it must be huge as space to forgive such a sinner as I am." That's one way and that's a good way—and probably that's the most popular way.

But there's another way to think of the grace of God. Think of it as the way God is—God being like God. And when God shows grace to a sinner He isn't being dramatic; He's acting like God. He'll never act any other way but like God. On the other hand, when that man whom justice has condemned turns his back on the grace of God in Christ and refuses to allow himself to be rescued, then the time comes when God must judge the man. And when God judges the man He acts like Himself in judging the man. When God shows love to the human race He acts like Himself. When God shows judgment to "the angels which kept not their first estate" (Jude 6), He acts like Himself.

Always God acts in conformity with the fullness of His own wholly perfect, symmetrical nature.

God always feels this overwhelming plentitude of goodness and He feels it in harmony with all His other attributes. There's no frustration in God. Everything that God is He is in complete harmony, and there is never any frustration in Him. But all this He bestows in His eternal Son.

A lot of people have talked about the goodness of God and then gotten sentimental about it and said, "God is too good to punish anybody," and so they have ruled out hell. But the man who has an adequate conception of God will not only believe in the love of God, but also in the holiness of God. He will not only believe in the mercy of God, but also in the justice of God. And when you see the everlasting God in His holy, perfect union, when you see the One God acting in judgment, you know that the man who chooses evil must never dwell in the presence of this holy God.

But a lot of people have gone too far and have written books and poetry that gets everybody believing that God is so kind and loving and gentle. God is so kind that infinity won't measure it. And God is so loving that He is immeasurably loving. But God is also holy and just.

Keep in mind that the grace of God comes only through Jesus Christ, and it is channeled only through Jesus Christ. The second Person of the Trinity opened the channel and grace flowed through. It flowed through from the day that Adam sinned all through Old Testament times, and it never flows any other way. So let's not write dreamy poetry about the goodness of our heavenly Father who is love— "love is God and God is love and love is all in all and all is God and everything will be OK." That's the summation of a lot of teaching these days. But it's false teaching.

Grace Is Released at the Cross

If I want to know this immeasurable grace, this overwhelming, astounding kindness of God, I have to step under the shadow of the cross. I must come where God releases grace. I must either look forward to it or I must look back at it. I must look one way or the other to that cross where Jesus died. Grace flowed out of His wounded side. The grace that flowed there saved Abel—and that same grace saves you. "No man cometh unto the Father, but by me," said our Lord Jesus Christ (John 14:6). And Peter said, "There is none other name under heaven given among men, whereby we must be saved," except the name of Jesus Christ (Acts 4:12).

The reason for that is, of course, that Jesus Christ is God. Law could come by Moses and only law could come by Moses. But grace came by Jesus Christ. And it came from the beginning. It could come only by Jesus Christ because there was no one else who was God who could die. No one else could take on Him flesh and still be the infinite God. And when Jesus walked around on earth and patted the heads of babies, forgave harlots and blessed mankind, He was simply God acting like God in a given situation. In everything that God does He acts like Himself.

But this one act of Jesus, this divine act, is also a human act. It couldn't have been a divine act alone, for it had to be for man. It couldn't have been a human act alone, for only God could save. It was a human act and a divine act. It was a historic act, a once-done act, done there in the darkness on the tree—hidden there, that secret act in darkness, never repeated. It was owned and accepted by God the Father Almighty who raised Him from the dead the third day and took Him to His own right hand.

So let's not degrade ourselves by vulgarizing the atonement. Over the last generation or two, some popular preachers have commercialized the atonement. They are good men and they've won some to Christ, and I thank God for everybody that's been won, but even while you're winning people to Christ, even winning them in great numbers, you can be so misleading and laying wrong emphasis that you start a trend that is bad.

These preachers have commercialized the atonement by giving us the doctrine of "paying a price." I believe He paid the price all right, and I can sing "Jesus paid it all, all to Him I owe," but we must not simplify it and illustrate it, or we vulgarize the atonement. I do not know how He did it. I can only stand as Ezekiel stood in the valley of dry bones and raise my head to God and say, "Oh Lord GOD, thou knowest" (37:3). Back there when the prophet said that He would come and give Himself a ransom for many, they didn't know quite what they were writing about, Peter says (see 1 Peter 1:10-11). And even angels watched the quill pens write over the old-fashioned paper the story of the coming Messiah. Looking over the shoulders of the prophets as they wrote, the angels desired to look into it (1:12). Not even the sharp-eyed angels around the throne of God know how He did it.

Some Things We Do Not Know

In secret, there in the dark, He did a once-done act never done before and never done again. And because He did that, the grace of God flows to all men. Let's remember that angels and prophets and even Paul said, "Without controversy great is the mystery of godliness: God was manifest in the flesh, justified in the Spirit, seen of angels, preached unto the Gentiles, believed on in the world, received up into glory" (1 Timothy 3:16). Many serious-minded, worthy scholars are ready to say that Paul's mind was the greatest that ever was known in the human race, except of course for the perfect mind of Christ. But this mighty mind never tried to understand it. He said, "Great is the mystery of godliness" (3:16), and that's all.

We're saved by His blood, but how are we saved by His blood? We're alive by His death, but why are we alive by His death? Atonement was made in His death, but how was atonement made in His death? Let's not vulgarize it by trying to understand it. But let's stand and gaze at the cross and say, "Oh Lord God, Thou knowest! Worthy is the Lamb that was slain!"

And if angels can be envious, they look upon us ransomed sinners and desire to look into it. But God says to the angels, the spirits there before the throne who can bear the burning bliss but who have never known a sinful world like this, "Go help My people." He sends them out to be ministering spirits to them who shall be heirs of salvation. But He never explains it to them. And I doubt whether there's an angel or archangel anywhere in heaven who understands what happened there on that cross.

We know He died; we know that because He died we don't have to. We know that He rose from the dead and because He rose from the dead, we who believe on Him will rise from the dead. We know He went to the right hand of God and sat down in perfect approval amidst the acclamations of the heavenly multitude. And we know that because He did we'll go there with Him. But why? God has shut up this secret in His own great heart forever. And we can only say, "Worthy is the Lamb."

Only Believe

Well, let's not try to understand, let's just believe. It was a hundred years before the Church ever began to try to explain the atonement. A hundred years! The fathers never tried; Paul never tried; Peter never tried. It was only when Greek influence came in that men began to try to think their way through it and give us explanations. And I appreciate those explanations. But for my part, I just stand and gaze on Him and say, "I don't know, I don't know!"

I don't know how He did it or what it all means any more than a two-year-old baby who stands gazing into her mother's face and says, "Mother, how did I get here?" Mother smiles and says, "You'll know later." She knows a two-year-old intellect won't understand. I think that when we say, "Oh God, how is it?" God will not say, "You will know later." I think He will say, "Believe on My Son." For what is of the earth He lets us know, but what is of heaven, He holds in His own great heart. And what He won't tell the angels, maybe He won't tell us.

Oh the wonder of it, the awesomeness of it! Can we preach too much about it? Can we sing too much about it? Can we pray too much, can we insist on it too much? Maybe we should cease to strain to understand, and we should just hear the story of grace told by the Lord of all grace and the fountain of all mercy, believed by the simple-hearted:

A certain man had two sons: and the younger of them said to his father, Father, give me the portion of goods that falleth to me. And he divided unto them his living. And not many days after the younger son gathered all together, and took his journey into a far country, and there wasted his substance with riotous living. And when he had spent all, there arose a mighty famine in that land. (Luke 15:11-14)

And this ungrateful boy, who had demanded his share before his father's death and thus had violated one of the tenderest conventions of human society, goes and asks for a job feeding hogs—and he was a Jew! Things got worse and worse and he had nothing and finally he had to push a hog away and try to eat some of the husks. And those who fed the hogs wouldn't give him any. They said, "Leave it alone—this is for the pigs." But he managed to stay alive.

Then one day he "came to himself " (15:17). He had been somebody else, but now he comes to himself. That's repentance! And he thinks about home, about Father, and he knew that Father hadn't changed. That's what Jesus was trying to tell us—the Father hasn't changed.

A long time ago, when I was in my early twenties, I'd heard the prodigal son was a backslider, but I didn't read it in the fifteenth chapter of Luke. He couldn't be a backslider and fit all the circumstances. I'd heard he was a sinner, but I couldn't hear God say of a sinner, "This, my son, was dead and is alive again." It didn't fit the circumstances.

So I went to God and I said, "God, will You show me?" Then I went to a place all by myself. Suddenly thee flashed over me the understanding, and I have never had reason to doubt

that this was God teaching me His Bible. I've
never heard anybody else say this, and I have-
n't made a lot of it. But God said to my heart,
*The prodigal son is neither a backslider nor a sin-
ner. The prodigal son is the human race; they
went out to the pigsty in Adam and came back in
Christ, My Son.*

There are two other parables there in Luke: the
Parable of the Lost Sheep and the Parable of the
Lost Coin. The sheep that wandered away was part
of the human race that would be saved, and when
he comes back he's the part of the human race that
is redeemed and will accept redemption. So those
of every race and color around the world that have
come back all come back in Christ. And they've all
come back in the person of that prodigal.

Do you know what they found the Father to be
like? They found He hadn't changed at all, in spite
of the insults, wrongs and his neighbors pitying
him, saying, "Oh, isn't it terrible the way that boy
treated his poor old dad?" His father was humili-
ated and shamed and sorry and grieved and heart-
broken, but when the boy came back, he hadn't
changed at all.

Jesus was saying to us, "You went away in
Adam, but you're coming back in Christ. And
when you come back you'll find the Father hasn't
changed. He's the same Father that He was when
you all went out, every man to his own way. But
when you come back in Jesus Christ you'll find
Him exactly the same as you left Him—un-
changed." And the Father ran and threw His arms

around him and welcomed him and put a robe and a ring on him and said, "This my son was dead, and is alive again" (15:24). This is the grace of God. Isn't it worth believing in, preaching, teaching, singing about while the world stands?

Where the Grace Is

If you're out of the grace of God, do you know where the grace is? Turn your eyes upon Jesus, and there's the grace of God flowing free for you—all the grace you need. If you set your teeth against Him, the grace of God might as well not exist for you. And Christ might as well not have died. But if you yield to Him and come home, then all the overwhelming, incomprehensible plentitude of goodness and kindness in the great illimitable reaches of God's nature are on your side. Even justice is on the side of the returning sinner: "He is faithful and just to forgive us our sins" (1 John 1:9). All the infinite attributes of God rejoice together when a man believes in the grace of God and returns home.

Father, we pray for all of us, that Thou wilt sweep away our self-righteousness, even any little, ragged traces of self-righteousness that may be left. Save us from ourselves. Let grace abound from Calvary, and teach us that it is not by grace and something else, but by grace alone, Thy goodness, Thy kindness in Christ Jesus. This we ask in the name of the Lord who loves us. Amen.

Chapter 7

God's Omnipresence

But will God indeed dwell on the earth? behold, the heaven and heaven of heavens cannot contain thee; how much less this house that I have builded? (1 Kings 8:27)

Am I a God at hand, saith the LORD, and not a God afar off? (Jeremiah 23:23)

That they should seek the Lord, if haply they might feel after him, and find him, though he be not far from every one of us: For in him we live, and move, and have our being. (Acts 17:27-28)

I have set the LORD always before me: because he is at my right hand, I shall not be moved. (Psalm 16:8)

Whither shall I go from thy spirit? or whither shall I flee from thy presence? If I ascend up into heaven, thou art there: if I make my bed in hell, behold, thou art there. If I take the wings of the morning, and dwell in the ut-

termost parts of the sea; Even there shall thy hand lead me, and thy right hand shall hold me. (Psalm 139:7-10)

These few texts certainly do not exhaust the great wealth of Scripture passages dealing with the topic of God's omnipresence. But I like to explain things by going behind everything to God Himself and showing that the teachings of the Holy Scriptures have their origin in the nature of God. They are what they are because God is what He is. These teachings rest upon the character of God and are guaranteed by the changeless attributes of the Lord God Almighty, the Ancient of Days.

What Omnipresence Is

I want to explain briefly what omnipresence is and then show what it means in human experience. That God is omnipresent is of course believed by all churches who believe in the Bible. I am not introducing anything new. Omnipresence means that God is all-present. God is close to (for that is what the word means—"close to, near to, here") everywhere. He is near to everything and everyone. He is here; He is next to you wherever you may be. And if you send up the furious question, "Oh God, where art Thou?" the answer comes back, "I am where you are; I am here; I am next to you; I am close to everywhere." That's what the Bible says.

There's reason to this as well as the evidence of

Scripture. If we had Scripture and no reason, we'd still believe it. But since we have Scripture to declare it and reason to shout, "It's true, I know it's true," then we may be sure that God is omnipresent. If there were any borders to God, if there were any place where God is not, then that place would mark the confines or the limits of God. And if God had limits, God could not be the infinite God. Some theologians call the infinitude of God His *immensity*, but that is not quite a big enough word. *Immensity* simply means that whatever you are talking about is hugely, vastly large. But *infinitude* means there isn't any way to say that God is large. Since He is infinite, then we can only say that God has no size at all; you cannot mea-sure God in any direction. God is infinite and perfect. Whenever you have finitude you have *creaturehood*, not God.

God is equally near to all parts of His universe. We think rightly about God and spiritual things only when we rule out the concept of space altogether. God, being infinite, does not dwell in space; He swallows up all space. Scripture says, "Do not I fill heaven and earth?" (Jeremiah 23:24) and that sounds as if God were contained in heaven and earth. But actually God fills heaven and earth just as the ocean fills a bucket which has been submerged in it a mile down. The bucket is full of the ocean, but the ocean surrounds the bucket in all directions. So when God says He fills heaven and earth, He does. But heaven and earth are submerged in God, and all

space is too. The "heaven of heavens cannot contain him" (2 Chronicles 2:6). God is not contained; God contains. And there is the difference.
"For in him we live, and move, and have our being" (Acts 17:28).

We talk about God being close to us or about
the problem of God being far away. We don't
think right because we think geographically or as-
tronomically; we think in light-years or meters or
inches or miles or leagues. We're thinking of Him
as dwelling in space, which He does not. Rather
He contains space so that space is in God. There
is never any problem about God being anywhere,
for the fact is, as the texts say, God is everywhere.

I believe what God says and leave those who do
not believe with the problems. Scripture says, "If I
ascend up into heaven, thou art there: if I make
my bed in hell, behold, thou art there" (Psalm
139:8). I don't understand it, but remember that
John Wesley said not to reject something just because you can't understand it. The omnipresence
of God requires that wherever there is anything—even hell—the presence of God must be.

Why is it, then, that the world thinks of God as
being infinitely remote, or as the song says, "far
away, beyond the starlit sky"? When the world
prays, as a rule they pray without any sense of
God's nearness at all. Always God is somewhere
else. Always God is far away. Why is this?

Our Remoteness from God

The reason is that in spiritual things closeness

and likeness are the same thing. Remoteness means dissimilarity.

When it comes to personality, when it comes to spirits, when it comes to that which is not material, distance doesn't mean anything. Jesus could go to the right hand of God the Father and still say to people on earth, "I am with you always" (Matthew 28:20) because Jesus Christ is God, and God being spirit can be instantaneously everywhere at the same time.

But we are shut off from God—not because God is spatially far from us, not because He is remote like a far galaxy or star, but because there is a dissimilarity in nature. When we think on spiritual things, we project our own human concepts on them. One of the challenges of the Bible teacher is to break down those human concepts, though not very many Bible teachers try to do it. One of the challenges of the Holy Spirit—if He has any challenges—is to get His people so spiritualized that they no longer think in material concepts.

For instance, your friends are the ones who are closest to you, and the closer the friend, the nearer that person is likely to be. But your enemy wants to put as much space between you and him as possible. So we tend to think of our friends as being near to us and our enemies as being far from us. As the world sees it, the farther away your enemy is, the better off you are, because you think in spatial terms.

That isn't the way we should think about God. There isn't any place you could go and not find

God. The psalmist says, "If I say, Surely the darkness shall cover me; even the night shall be light about me. Yea, the darkness hideth not from thee; but the night shineth as the day: the darkness and the light are both alike to thee" (Psalm 139:11-12). There isn't anywhere that we can go because "Thou knowest my downsitting and mine uprising, thou understandest my thought afar off" (139:2). We do not have the problem of distance or remoteness when we come to God. What makes this a Christian assembly is that God is here.

Two creatures may be in the same room and yet be millions of miles apart. For instance, if it were possible to put an ape and an angel in the same room, there would be no compatibility, no communion, no understanding, no friendship; there would be only distance. The shining angel and the slobbering, gibbering ape would be far, far removed from each other. When we come to anything that is intellectual or spiritual or of the soul, space, matter, weight and time have no meaning at all.

That is why I can stand and smile at all the "space boys." They tell us that if you could accelerate a twelve-inch ruler to the speed of light, it would loose its length and not have any length at all—it would be "lengthless." Did you know that? That information is supposed to knock you for a loop and cause you to quit praying. It doesn't stop me from praying, because I don't think in spatial terms. I don't think in terms of speed or distance, because God, being spirit, is right here. And He'll never be any farther away, and He can't get any nearer than He is right now.

The reason we sense that God is remote is because there is a dissimilarity between moral characters. God and man are dissimilar now. God made man in His image, but man sinned and became unlike God in his moral nature. And because he is unlike God, communion is broken. Two enemies may hate each other and be separated and apart even though they are for a moment forced to be together. There is an alienation there—and that is exactly what the Bible calls that moral incompatibility between God and man.

God is not far away in distance, but He seems to be because He is far away in character. He is unlike man because man has sinned and God is holy. The Bible has a word for this moral incompatibility, this spiritual unlikeness between man and God—alienation.

The book of Ephesians tells us what it is that gives to the world that sense of God being "far away, beyond the starlit sky":

And you hath he quickened, who were dead in trespasses and sins; wherein in time past ye walked according to the course of this world, according to the prince of the power of the air, the spirit that now worketh in the children of disobedience: among whom also we all had our conversation in times past in the lusts of our flesh, fulfilling

the desires of the flesh and of the mind; and
were by nature the children of wrath, even
as others. (Ephesians 2:1-3)

Then in the fourth chapter we read:

This I say therefore, and testify in the
Lord, that ye henceforth walk not as other
Gentiles walk, in the vanity of their mind,
having the understanding darkened, being
alienated from the life of God through the
ignorance that is in them, because of the
blindness of their heart: who being past feeling have given themselves over unto lasciviousness, to work all uncleanness with
greediness. (4:17-19)

Could these verses describe Jesus, who is God
incarnated, who is in character all that God is,
perfectly? No! They describe the alienated sinner,
having his understanding darkened. Do they describe the glorious Son of God—ignorant, blind in
heart, past feeling, given over to lasciviousness,
walking in uncleanness and greediness? Of course
not! They describe exactly the opposite of Jesus.
    These verses show that the sinner is so dissimilar
to God that the distance is one of character, not
space. God is not one inch away from a sinner. And
yet He is far from the sinner. Am I contradicting
myself? Not at all! Since God is omnipresent—close to anywhere, next to everywhere—then
the distance is that of character, not space.

When the sinner prays, "Oh God, save me and forgive me for Jesus' sake," he does not call God down from His high throne. *God is already there.* And he knows at that moment that God is there. But it's a dissimilarity of character that makes the difference.

Suppose a very, very godly man and a very licentious, abandoned, evil man were forced to sit together on a journey. What could they talk about? They'd have to find some common ground, and it might be the landscape or the pretty tree over there or something, but they could never have fellowship. They might if the sinner listened to the urgent witness of the good man. But as long as the sinner shut himself off and said, "You can't talk to me about God," there would be no communion. They would be miles apart even though they were the same nationality, same age and traveling in the same vehicle.

So it is with God and man. God is away from man, and man is away from God, and that's why the world searches after God "if haply they might . . . find him" (Acts 17:27). They don't find Him because God and man are dissimilar in their moral natures. God is in perfect holiness, man in perfect iniquity, and the two can never meet. That's why God seems so far away.

Illustrations from Scripture

When Adam sinned he ran and hid himself from the presence of God. I heard a Jewish rabbi talking the other night on the radio, and he said that once a very godly Jewish rabbi was in jail. The jailer was interested in the old man. He went to the rabbi and said, "Rabbi, I've got a theological question I'd like to ask you, out of your own Bible. Do you believe God knows everything?"

"Oh, certainly," said the rabbi.

"Well, how is it then that God said, `Adam, where art thou?' If God knew where he was, why did He ask?"

"Well, son," the rabbi said, "that's not hard. God said, `Adam, where art thou?' not because He didn't know where Adam was, but because Adam didn't know where he was. The question was asked of Adam. Adam was lost, not God."

God knew where Adam was, but Adam didn't know where he was. Adam was alienated from God, and I think the old rabbi had the explanation right. Similarly, in Genesis 18:21 God said, "I will go down now, and see," but that didn't mean God was coming down to get information like a newspaper reporter. The great God knows everything in one instantaneous, perfect act. And yet He comes down among us and acts like us and says, "I will go down and see."

When Jonah refused to obey God and broke off and alienated his heart, he got in a ship to get away from the presence of God. He thought he could get away from God. How foolish of him to think he could get away from God! Then there was Peter, who knelt down and said, "Depart from me; for I am a sinful man, O Lord" (Luke 5:8).

It is the heart that puts distance between us and

God. We must not think of God as being far away, for the reason that God does not dwell in space and "the heaven of heavens cannot contain Him" (2 Chronicles 2:6), but He contains the heaven of heavens. And therefore God is near to you now—nearer to you than you are to yourself.

And yet the sinner is far from God. He isn't far from God—and yet he is. God is not far away like a Roman god up on a holy mountain. God is far away in His holy unlikeness to everything sinful. He's far away in the sense of alienation and enmity. The natural man cannot please God (see Romans 8:8), for God and man are alienated. This is the terrible law of the world: alienation.

The Bliss of Moral Creatures

Because God cannot in His holy heaven have beings who are morally dissimilar to Himself, there has to be a place to put those who refuse to become like God. We must be like Him to enter there; we shall see Him and shall be like Him, says the Holy Spirit in First John 3:2. This—the presence of God—is the bliss of all moral creatures. Our fathers called it the Vision Beatific.

Just as the shining of the sun is the bliss of all creatures that love the sun, and they come out of hiding to fly or crawl or swim when the sun returns, so the presence of that Holy God is the bliss of all moral creatures. And the absence of it is the terror and grief and sorrow of all fallen creatures. I am not talking about God's presence, but God's *manifest* presence. There's a vast difference.

The presence of God is even in hell, the Holy Spirit says in Psalm 139, but His manifest presence is only in heaven and where good souls are. Therefore, we are so close to God that He can hear our slightest whisper—and yet a person can have such a sense of alienation and remoteness that he or she will go to the river and commit suicide, thinking there's no God in the universe anywhere.

This accounts for our busy activities; it accounts for practically all the entertainment in the world. People invent every sort of entertainment because they can't live with themselves knowing they're alienated from God. They can't live knowing that there is a moral dissimilarity that shall forever and forever keep a sense of all but infinite remoteness between their soul and their God who is their life and their sunshine.

If there were no fire in hell, and no "worm [that] dieth not" (Mark 9:48), hell would be hell enough, because moral creatures are cut off forever from the sunshine of God's face. And if there were no golden streets, no jasper walls, no angels, no harps, no living creatures, no elders and no sea of glass, heaven would be heaven enough, because we shall see His face and His name shall be on our foreheads.

It is the manifest, conscious presence of God that makes heaven heaven. And it is the refusal of God ever to manifest His presence to those who do not want to be good that makes hell what it is and makes the world what it is. If God were to manifest Himself to people all over the earth, every nightclub would be emptied or would turn into a happy prayer meeting. Every house of ill fame would be emptied in five minutes, and everyone with deep repentance and sorrow of heart would be down on his knees before God asking for forgiveness and weeping tears of happiness. It is the presence of God that gives bliss to moral creatures and the absence of God that brings everlasting woe to moral creatures.

People deny the sun and still want a bright day. So they invent every kind of light imaginable and whirl all kinds of Roman candles over their heads to get a little light. We call that entertainment, the theater and all the rest. It helps people to forget that they are without God.

Human nature is so dissimilar to God's nature that it creates a remote, everlasting, unbridgeable gulf. The Ethiopian cannot change his skin nor the leopard his spots (see Jeremiah 13:23)—in other words, the person born in sin can't get out of it. God will never change and man can't change himself. How then can God and the human race ever come together?

The Reconciliation of the Dissimilar

The dissimilarity can be reconciled only by One who is both God and man. The man cannot educate himself into a likeness of God and he cannot cultivate himself into a likeness of God. He can begin to go to art galleries and read Shakespeare and visit the opening nights at the opera, and begin to drop his "r's" and open his "a's" and sound very "cultured"—but when it's all over he's still inwardly what he was before, walking in the vanity of his mind, blinded by the ignorance that is within him, cut off from the life of God "having no hope, and without God in the world" (Ephesians 2:12).

Man can't right himself. Religions have tried it, philosophies have tried it, school systems have tried it, the police try it. We try everywhere to bring a similarity that God will recognize so that instead of our having that sense of infinite remoteness, we can say with Jacob, "Surely the LORD is in this place" (Genesis 28:16). But we can't get it. How can it be done?

It says in Second Corinthians 5:19 that "God was in Christ, reconciling." God's love in Christ was reconciling. How can God reconcile the dissimilar nature of man to His own? Reconciliation can be done in two ways:

One way it can be accomplished is by the two parties who are alienated compromising and thus getting together. If this man and I had four propositions that were keeping us apart, we might get together and pray and say, "I don't want to be out of friendship with you, and therefore I'll make a concession on this." And he'd say, "Well, all right then, I'll make a concession on this." If he moves halfway and I move halfway, we would be reconciled.

But how can God say to the sinner, "I'll move over halfway"? Can He say, "You're blind, so I'll move over and be half blind, and you'll move over and be half blind. You're dead and I'll move over and be half dead, and you'll move over and be half dead"? And thus by God coming halfway and compromising Himself, could He and man be reconciled? To do that God would have to void His Godhead and cease to be God.

I'd rather go to hell than go to a heaven presided over by a god who would compromise with sin, and I believe every true man and woman would feel the same. We want God to be the holy God that He is. God can never compromise; it doesn't work that way. The prodigal son and his father did not meet halfway to the far country. The boy came clear back where he belonged. And so the sinner in his repentance comes all the way back to God, and God doesn't move from His holy position of infinite holiness, righteousness and loveliness, world without end.

God never compromises and comes halfway down. God stays the God that He is. This is the God we adore—our faithful, unchangeable Friend whose love is as great as His power and knows neither limit nor end. We don't want God to compromise. We don't want God to wink at our iniquity. We want God to do something about it.

What did He do about it? He came down and became flesh and became both God and man, sin excepted, in order that by His death He might remove everything out of the way so that man could come back. He couldn't come back if Christ had not come and died. But now because He came and died, He removed every moral obstacle out of the way so man can come home.

Peter, approaching it from another direction, says that God has left us the promises of the gospel, "that by these ye might be partakers of the divine nature" (2 Peter 1:4). What does that mean? It means that when the sinner comes home, repents and believes on Christ savingly, God implants in the heart of that previous sinner some of His own nature. And then the nature in God and the nature in the sinner are no longer dissimilar, but are one. The sinner is home and the dissimilarity is gone; the unlikeness is removed. The nature of God implanted in man now makes it morally proper that man and God should have fellowship.

Without compromising Himself in any way, God now receives the returning sinner and puts a deposit of His own nature and life in that sinner. That's what the new birth is. It's not joining a church, not being baptized, not quitting this or that bad habit, though everybody will quit his bad habits. The new birth is an implantation of divine life.

To go back to my own rather awkward illustration, the ape and the angel are in the same room, staring at each other. There's no getting them together. How could you do it? If the great God Almighty would deposit the glorious celestial nature of the angel in the ape, the ape would leap to his feet and shake hands with the angel and call him by name, because similarity would instantly be there. But as long as one has the nature of an ape and the other of an angel, there can be nothing but everlasting dissimilarity.

In the same way, the world with all its money, culture, education, science and philosophy is still a moral ape. The Bible has said so. The holy God cannot compromise Himself to fellowship and neither can that man understand God, for the natural man cannot understand God and there can be no fellowship.

But God moved in Christ and died on a cross and so took the obstacles away. By the new birth, He gives some of His own delightful, divine nature to the sinner. And the sinner looks up and says, "Abba, Father" (Romans 8:15, Galatians 4:6) for the first time in his or her life. Now he or she is converted.

That's what happened to Jacob. He was converted in Genesis 28 when he saw the ladder to heaven, and he was filled with the Holy Spirit in Genesis 32 at the Jabbok River—two works of grace. He was an old sinner with the name Jacob, which meant "a supplanter"; he was crooked.

And Jacob went out from Beersheba, and went toward Haran. And he lighted upon a certain place, and tarried there all night, because the sun was set; and he took of the stones of that place, and put them for his pillows, and lay down in that place to sleep. And he dreamed, and behold a ladder set up on the earth, and the top of it reached to heaven: and behold the angels of God ascending and descending on it. (28:10-12)

And God and Jacob met and Jacob believed in his God. "And Jacob awaked out of his sleep, and he said, Surely the LORD is in this place; and I knew it not. And . . . this is the gate of heaven" (28:16-17). It was as much the gate of heaven when he lay down as when he awoke. But he said, "I didn't know it." The presence of God had been there all the time, but now by a work of God, he got the *conscious* presence of God.

Communion with God

That's why a soundly converted sinner, who has a conscious transplantation of the divine nature into his heart by faith in Jesus Christ, is likely to be explosively happy. He says with Jacob, "This is the gate of heaven. God is in this place and I didn't know it." God's conscious presence has been restored to him.

What makes heaven heaven? The unhindered, unsullied presence of God! What makes hell hell? The absence of a consciousness of the presence of God! That's the difference between a prayer meeting and a dance hall. The omnipresent God fills heaven and earth, contains heaven and earth and is present everywhere. But in the prayer meeting some little old lady kneels and says, "Oh Jesus, where two or three are gathered Thou art there in the midst" (see Matthew 18:20). God is there. In the dance hall they'd be embarrassed if the presence of God were to be manifest.

That's why conversions are such milk-and-water things these days. We pick them out of their shell and try rubbing their nose in red-letter texts to make them think they're converted. They've not had an implantation of the divine life—there's no similarity—and therefore God and man do not meet in the bush. But wherever God and man meet, there's the joyous rebound of the human spirit. Similarity is restored, and instead of God being a million light-years away, the man can hardly believe his own heart when he cries, "Oh, God is in this place and I didn't know it."

Ah, for some of the old conversions again. I've not seen too many of that kind, but I've seen a few—conversions where a man would kneel in bursts of tears and agony, confess his sins to God, believe on Jesus Christ and get to his feet with a light on his face and walk around shaking hands with everybody, keeping back the tears the best he can and smiling through the tears he can't keep back. What causes that kind of conversion is not only the conscious taking away of sin, but the conscious presence of God revealed to the heart inside.

That's the joy of conversion—not bringing God from some distant star, but knowing God by a change of nature.

Chapter 8

God's Immanence

> *But will God indeed dwell on the earth? behold, the heaven and heaven of heavens cannot contain thee; how much less this house that I have builded? (1 Kings 8:27)*
>
> *That they should seek the Lord, if haply they might feel after him, and find him, though he be not far from every one of us: for in him we live, and move, and have our being. (Acts 17:27-28)*
>
> *Whither shall I go from thy spirit? or whither shall I flee from thy presence? If I ascend up into heaven, thou art there: if I make my bed in hell, behold, thou art there. If I take the wings of the morning, and dwell in the uttermost parts of the sea; even there shall thy hand lead me, and thy right hand shall hold me. (Psalm 139:7-10)*

God is omnipresent, which means God is everywhere. God is also immanent, which means that God *penetrates* everything.

This is standard Christian doctrine, believed even in the earliest days of Judaism. God is omnipresent and immanent, penetrating everything even while He contains all things. The bucket that is sunk into the depths of the ocean is full of the ocean. The ocean is in the bucket, but also the bucket is in the ocean—surrounded by it. This is the best illustration I can give of how God dwells in His universe and yet the universe dwells in God.

In the previous chapter I dealt with the fact of remoteness—that distance is unlikeness—and I pointed out that hell is for those unlike God. The moral dissimilarity creates hell. For those beings who are morally dissimilar to God, hell is their final place. For those creatures who are morally similar to God, with some likeness to God, heaven is their place because their nature belongs there. Reconciliation to God is secured by three divine acts: atonement, justification and regeneration.

Atonement, of course, is the objective work of Christ. It is what He did on the cross before any of us now living were living. It is something He did alone in the dark. It is objective; that is, it's outside of us. It did not take place inside of anybody. It took place objectively, externally. The spear went into His side alone and He suffered. The nails were in His hands and feet. That's atonement.

It could have been done without affecting anybody; it was done, and still there are millions who have died unaffected by it. But here is the beauty of it, that this act which He did in the darkness there makes justification possible.

Justification is the second act which God does to reconcile men to Himself. Justification is that which declares the sinner righteous, and that also is external to us—that is, it doesn't reach us. Justified persons may be no better off for their justification if that's all that happened to them, because justification is a legal thing. They may stand before a court and be declared innocent of a crime, but it doesn't change them. They weigh exactly the same they did as before, and they have the same relationships. They are in every way the same people they were before, except that they are judicially freed, declared not guilty before the law.

It could have a subjective effect if they found it out and rejoiced, but the work is not done in them. The work is done in the minds of the jurors and before the law. It's a judicial thing. So justification is the second act that God performs to get us reconciled with Him.

The third act is regeneration. Regeneration, of course, takes place at the same time justification takes place. I said that when God justifies a person, that person could be justified and not be any better off. That is technically possible but not actually so, because when God justifies a person He also regenerates the person. Nobody was ever justified and not regenerated. You can think of them separately, though actually you cannot separate them.

Justification and regeneration are not the same.

This is the most ordinary, basic Christian theology that everyone ought to know. Regeneration takes place within the life of the person, within the heart of the person. It's a subjective thing; it deals with a person's nature. It gets inside the person. Because Jesus died in the darkness and because God accepted that as atonement for our sin, if we believe in Christ, God can justify us, declare us righteous and then regenerate us by imparting to us the nature of God. For God tells us that it is through these promises that we are "partakers of the divine nature" (2 Peter 1:4).

Restoration of Moral Comparability

A regenerated person is someone who has partaken of the divine nature, who has a new relationship to God which gives that person eternal life. This reunites God and the person and restores some degree of moral likeness to the person. The newest convert who was born again today (*born again* and *regenerate* have the same meaning) has a degree of moral likeness to God which gives a measure of comparability.

Heaven is a place of complete comparability, and sin introduces incompatibility between God and the sinner. There cannot be any comparability or communion between the two because sin introduces that quality which throws humans and God out of accord with each other. But when a sinner believes in the blood of the atonement and puts his or her trust in Christ, he or she is justified in heaven and regenerated on earth. Earth is the only place you get regenerated—don't wait until you die, because there's no place to regenerate after you're dead!

When you trust in Christ, you're regenerated; you're given a measure of the character of God, so that there is enough of the image restored that there can be quite a full measure of comparability. And that comparability allows God to draw feelingly near to a person. And it makes communion morally consistent.

You can't have communion where there is complete unlikeness. You may pet the head of a dog, but you can't commune with the dog; there's too great a dissimilarity of nature. In the same way, God cannot commune with a sinner because there is a violent unlikeness, a dissimilarity that makes communion impossible.

But it says in Colossians 3:10, "Put on the new man, which is renewed in knowledge after the image of him that created him." That new man within you is the regenerated man—the new man who is you, started on your way toward Godlikeness. And there is enough of it there, even in the new convert, that God can commune without incongruity.

God, being the God He is, can never commune with anything except His own likeness. And where there is no likeness there can be no fellowship between God and that unlike thing. The verse says we have "put on the new man." These Colossian Christians were not perfect by a long way, but they had put on the new man. The seed that was in them, the root of the matter, was in their hearts. They were regenerated so God could commune with His own image in them and see a little bit of His own face there and hold communion with His people. That's why we can say, "Abba, Father" (Romans 8:15, Galatians 4:6).

A young father goes to the hospital to see his newborn heir. He looks through the glass, and there never was a father yet who wasn't excited, frightened, bewildered—and disappointed. His eyes run over all twenty-five or fifty babies in the nursery, and he picks a pretty one and hopes that's his. Then when they turn the thing around and he sees that it isn't, he's disappointed.

But when people tell the father, "He's the very image of you," the father beams! Actually it isn't much of a compliment—the little thing is a blob of squirm and suck and wiggle and red skin and no hair. Yet there is a little bit of likeness there; there is a similarity.

In a deeper way, a new convert, the fellow that's just been born again, certainly may not be much like God, but he has something of the resemblance of the deity, and so God can own him as His. The angels can recognize a family resemblance.

Why then this serious problem among real Christians—this feeling that God is far away or that we are far away from God? It's hard to rejoice if you're suffering from that sense of remoteness.

I believe that most Christians do suffer from a sense of divine remoteness. They know God is with them and they're sure they're God's children. They can take you to their marked New Testament and prove to you seriously and soberly that they're justified and regenerated, that they belong to God, that heaven is going to be their home and that Christ is their Advocate above. They've got the theology; they know all this in their head, but they're suffering from a sense of remoteness.

To know something in your head is one thing; to feel it in your heart is another. And I think most Christians are trying to be happy without having a sense of the Presence. It's like trying to have a bright day without having the sun. You could say, "According to my watch, it is fifteen minutes past noon, and therefore the sun is up. Let us rejoice in the sun. Isn't it beautiful and bright? Let us take it by faith and rejoice that the sun is up, that all is well and the sun is up."

You can point upward and say, "The sun is up," but you're kidding yourself. As long as it's dark, gloomy and rainy, and the wet soggy leaves keep dribbling down, you're not having a bright day. But when the sun comes out, you can rejoice in the presence of the sun.

Yearning for God

Now most Christians are theological Christians. They know they are saved; somebody's given them a marked New Testament and it's proper that we should until they get their theology straight. But they're trying to be happy without a sense of the Presence. The sense of the Presence is absent and that yearning you see is a desire to be nearer to God.

You'll find that yearning in two places: prayers and hymns. If you think that I am merely spinning this out of my head, go to the next prayer meeting and kneel down with the brethren and listen to them pray. They all pray alike. "Oh Lord, come; oh Lord, draw near; oh Lord, show Thyself; be near to me, Lord." If that isn't enough, hear us sing "Come, Thou Fount of Every Blessing" or "Draw Me Nearer, Nearer, Nearer, Blessed Lord."

The yearning to be near to God and have God come nearer to us is universal among born-again Christians. And yet we think of God as coming from across distance to us, when the Bible and Christian theology, all the way back to David, declare that God is already here—now. God doesn't dwell in space, and therefore God doesn't have to come like a ray of light from some remote place. There is no remote place in God; He contains all remoteness and all distances in His own great heart.

Why then do we feel Him in the distance? It's the dissimilarity in our natures; it's the unlikeness. We've got enough likeness that God can commune with us and call us His children and we can say, "Abba, Father." But in the practical working out of it, we sense our dissimilarity, and that is why God seems remote.

What I'm trying to get across is simply this: nearness to God is not a geographical or an astronomical thing. It is not a spatial thing. It is a spiritual thing, having to do with nature. And so when we pray "God, draw me nearer," or "God, come nearer," we're not praying (if we're good theologians) for God to come down from some remote distance. We know God's here now. Jesus said, "Lo, I am with you always" (Matthew 28:20). The Lord is here. Jacob said, "God is in this place and I didn't know it" (see Genesis 28:16). He didn't say, "God came to this place"; he said, "God is in this place."

What are we praying for, then? We are praying for a manifestation of the presence of God. Not the presence, but the *manifestation* of the presence. Why don't we have the manifestation? Because we allow unlikenesses. We allow moral dissimilarity. That "sense" of absence is the result of the remaining unlikeness within us.

This desire, this yearning to be near to God is, in fact, a yearning to be like Him. It's the yearning of the ransomed heart to be like God so there can be perfect communion, so the heart and God can come together in a fellowship that is divine.

There is a similarity which makes it compatible and proper for God to commune with His children—even the poorest and weakest of His children. But there are also dissimilarities, such that there isn't the degree of fellowship that there ought to be. There isn't that perfection of the sense of God's presence that we want and yearn and pray for and sing about.

How are we going to know what God is like so that we may know whether we're like God? The answer is: God is like Christ, for Christ is God manifest to mankind. By looking at our Lord Jesus we will know what God is like and will know what we have to be like to experience the unbroken and continuous presence of God.

The presence is here, but the sense of the presence is absent. We know the sun is there, even though the clouds are hanging so low we can reach up and touch them. Even when we know the sun is there in mid-heaven, we have to turn our car headlights on for safety. Because there are clouds in the way, we don't feel or see the sun, but we know it's there.

And we Christians know God is here, but there is a sense of His absence. A man feels the sun is gone never to return; he knows better, yet he can't be happy because he can't see the sun. We feel that God is away even when we know that He is present, and He can't manifest Himself as He wants to for certain reasons.

The Holiness of Christ

Let's note some of the qualities of Jesus. The first one, of course, is holiness. Our God is holy and our Lord is holy, and we call the Spirit the Holy Spirit. Now think how stained and how spotted and how carnal the average Christian is. We allow stains—months go by without repentance. Years go by without asking for cleansing or taking it. Then we sing, "Draw me nearer, nearer, nearer, blessed Lord." Or we pray, "Come, Lord, come to this meeting." Well, the Lord is there.

What we're praying is, "Oh Lord, show Thyself," but the Lord cannot; a holy God cannot show Himself in full communion to an unholy Christian. You ask, "Is it possible to be a Christian and be unholy?" It's possible to be a carnal Christian. You can have the seed of God in you, be regenerated and justified and still be unholy in some of your inner feelings and desires and willingness.

The Unselfishness of Christ

The second quality is unselfishness. Do you notice that Jesus Christ was completely unselfish and gave Himself? But how self-centered and self-indulgent most Christians are! Even when they're reading books on revival, they're still self-centered. Even when they're praying for revival, they're still self-indulgent. A revival is, among other things, a sudden manifestation. It's a breaking of the sun through the clouds. It's not the coming of the sun; it's the breaking of the sun through the clouds.

I'm sick in my own heart, sick about myself, sick about my friends, sick about the preachers and their ministry. How utterly self-centered we can become. We live for self, talk loudly about glorifying God and boast and say, "This is to the glory of God"—and yet we are self-centered. You'll know you're self-centered if anybody crosses you and your hackles go up. Don't smile about it. It's not funny—it's serious!

There's enough money, potentially, in the average congregation not only to keep the church going but to double the missionary offering. There would be enough—if we weren't so self-indulgent. Of course, a perfectly selfless Christ who gave Himself and poured Himself out and had no selfishness can't warm up to the Christian heart that is self-indulgent and self-centered. He loves us; He's our Shepherd; He's our Advocate above, who pleads our cause in heaven. We're His brethren in Christ and God His Father is our Father. But our selfishness prevents us from enjoying the fellowship, the sweetness that changes some people into saints while they walk on earth (and I mean *saint* in more than a technical sense).

The Love of Christ

The third quality is love. He so loved that He gave all. But how calculating so many of us are! We say, "Well, I can go to this meeting but I can't go to that one; the doctor has told me not to overdo it." So we have it all figured out. We put our spiritual life on a budget. We won't spend anything for God unless we can justify it in the columns of our budget. What a cheap, carnal way of living, and yet it's true—we do it! How narrow God's people are.

The love of the Lord Jesus Christ was a great, passionate, outpoured thing that caused Him to give Himself completely. It is said, "Christ pleased not himself " (Romans 15:3). Even our Lord pleased not Himself. But do you know what is wrong with us? We are self-pleasers. We live for ourselves.

There are people who would buy a new car even if it meant their church went broke and had to close its doors. There are women who would dress in the latest style even if the mission cause died and every missionary had to be sent home. Yet we're saints, we're born-again, we're believers—we have our marked New Testament!

We may be Christians, but the love we have is a calculating and narrow love, a love that doesn't give itself. And so how can He who gave Himself ever fellowship with us? Do you want a Bible illustration of this? Let me give it to you. It is in the fifth chapter of the Song of Solomon, that delicate, gentle, wondrous, beautiful book of which Dr. Scofield said, "Sin has almost deprived us of the ability to kneel before that burning bush."

You'll remember that the bridegroom (who represents Jesus) had given gifts to his bride-to-be. He was out taking care of his sheep, out among the lilies. The dew was falling, and his locks were wet with the dews of the night (5:2). He was out there doing what his interests required him to do, what his heart wanted to do.

He came and knocked on her door to say, "Won't you come and join me?" She said, "How can I? I am not dressed for it. I'm dressed for the couch and the home, and even my hands drip with the ointments you've given me. I can't come." And so he disappeared (5:3-6). He was still her lover and he still wanted to marry her (and he did finally, thank God, and it came out all right).

He was out there pouring himself out, and she

was in her house admiring herself and taking long whiffs of the perfume that he'd given her, standing before the mirror and admiring the robes and jewelry he'd given her. He wanted her, but she wanted his jewelry and his perfumes. Then finally she got under conviction about it and she quickly, hastily dressed, not really for street dress. But she got some clothes on and a robe about her and started out looking for her beloved.

She asked the watchman, "Where is he?" And the watchman beat her (5:7) and said she was a harlot and told her to go home. She went on staggering under the blows and couldn't find him. And while she was hunting him, her friends said, "What's the matter? Why don't you go home?" They said, "What is thy beloved more than another beloved?" (5:9). And then she burst out into a beautiful song of praise, saying, "My beloved is white and ruddy"—she described him from head to foot—"the chiefest among ten thousand" (5:10).

He wanted her fellowship and she was too selfish and self-centered. Of course there could be no fellowship while he's out there doing one thing and she's selfishly staying in the house doing another.

Other Qualities of Christ

Another quality of Christ is kindness. Think how utterly kind our Lord Jesus is. The love of God is kinder than the measure of man's mind. Think of the kindness of Jesus in contrast to the harshness, the severity, the sharpness, the bitterness, the acidity in so many people's lives. How can a kind Savior feel perfectly at home with a harsh Christian?

Then there is forgiveness. He is a forgiving Lord and He forgave them while they beat Him. He forgave them while they put Him on the cross. But how hard and vengeful so many of the Lord's children are! Can you remember bad things that happened to you twenty years ago? You can't get over it; you say you've forgiven it, but you haven't. You're vengeful; He is forgiving. And He proved He was forgiving by dying in blood. You prove that you're vengeful and hard by many proofs and demonstrations.

Then think of the zeal of Jesus. "The zeal of thine house hath eaten me up" (Psalm 69:9). Think of the zeal of God. "The zeal of the LORD of hosts will perform this" (Isaiah 9:7). The most zealous thing I know is fire. Wherever fire burns it burns with hot zeal. And the heart of Jesus was like that. But think of the lukewarm Christian, of Christians who haven't been to a prayer meeting in years, of the careless and torpid Christian—the torpor that lies over the Church of God.

Then there is the humility of Jesus. Though He was the highest, He came down and acted like the lowest. And though we are the lowest we sometimes act the proudest and the most arrogant. How completely unlike Jesus, how unlike God.

Likeness Is Not Justification

Am I saying we are justified by being like God? I hope I've made it clear that we are justified by be-

ing declared righteous by Almighty God, who bases
His sentence upon the cross of Jesus and the dying
of the Savior in the darkness there on the hill. Then
because He made atonement, God justifies. And
when He justifies, He regenerates. You're saved by
justification and regeneration.

But regeneration does not perfect the image of
God in you. The image of God must continue to
grow and come forth, as an artist works on a
painting. First it's only an outline and a general
confusion, but the artist knows what's there, and
slowly it comes out. And so God seems far from
us because we're so unlike God.

Horace Bushnell and his friend went out on the
hill to pray and sat and talked about God until
slowly sunset and the stars came out and the
darkness settled around while they sat on the
grass. Then before they left, Bushnell said,
"Brother, let us pray before we go." So there in the
darkness, Bushnell lifted up his heart to God, and
his friend said afterward, "I pulled my arms in
tight around me. I was afraid to reach them out
lest I touch God."

I once knelt under an apple tree in a field with
several other preachers and a Salvation Army
man, Captain Ireland. We all prayed and then as
Captain Ireland began to pray, I suddenly sensed
a nearness. There was another One there who
hadn't come out, but He'd been there all the time.
"Am I a God at hand, saith the LORD, and not a
God afar off?" (Jeremiah 23:23).

How can He continually manifest His presence

to the proud and the arrogant when He is so humble and low? To the lukewarm and the careless when He is so zealous? To the hard and the vengeful when He is so forgiving? To the harsh and severe when He is so kind? To the calculating when His love led Him to die? When we are so stained, how can we have fellowship with Him?

And then the heavenly mindedness of Jesus, oh think of that! He was with the Father, in the bosom of the Father while He was on earth. He said, "The only begotten Son, which is in the bosom of the Father" (John 1:18). Notice it says *is*, not *was*—He never left the bosom of the Father while He was on earth. The only time He left it was in that awful wrenching agony when God turned away from Him on the cross that He might die for mankind. But never at any other time.

He talked about the other world: "I am from above" (John 8:23); "I came down from heaven" (6:38). He lived in the heart of God and the other world and the world above was the world which He inhabited. And think how earthly His people are and how worldly. They talk of furniture, TV sets, baseball, football, automobiles, picture windows, split-level houses, politics—anything but heaven and God.

Then we want to pray, "Draw me nearer, nearer." You're as near as you can get as far as distance is concerned. But He can't manifest Himself because there is a dissimilarity of nature. You have enough of His nature that you're justified and regenerated, but you haven't enough to per-

fect the fellowship. The perfection of the fellowship—this is what we need so desperately.

There was a man once who followed the Lord
afar off. But he couldn't live with it. Some of you
have learned to live with it. You've gotten older
and you've learned to live in the twilight and not
mind it. You've learned to live in the chill and not
mind it. What can I do for you? How can I help
you? I know no way. Peter followed afar off but
he couldn't stand it, and the Lord turned and
looked at him. Then Peter went outside and wept
bitterly.

Have you any tears for your unlikeness? Have
you any tears for that distance between you and
God that you know isn't there and yet feel is
there? You're not diminishing in any way the
things God has already done in your life. You're
grateful and thankful for every blessing, for justification, for the good grace of God on your life.
But you can't escape that sense of remoteness, and
many a day is a heavy one because God seems far
from you. You know He isn't but you feel He is.
He can't show His face. You've allowed
self-indulgence, harshness, a vengeful spirit, lukewarmness, pride and worldliness to put a cloud
over the face of God.

I think that repentance is called for. We need to
repent of unlikeness; of unholiness in the presence of the holy; of self-indulgence in the presence of the selfless Christ; of harshness in the
presence of the kind Christ; of hardness in the
presence of the forgiving Christ; of lukewarmness

in the presence of the zealous Christ, burning like a fiery flame; of worldliness and earthliness in the presence of the heavenly Christ. I think we ought to repent.

What are you going to do about it? Has He opened your heart?

Chapter 9

God's Holiness

Who is like unto thee, O LORD, among the gods? who is like thee, glorious in holiness? (Exodus 15:11)

Behold, he putteth no trust in his saints; yea, the heavens are not clean in his sight. (Job 15:15)

Behold even to the moon, and it shineth not; yea, the stars are not pure in his sight. How much less man, that is a worm? (Job 25:5-6)

But thou art holy, O thou that inhabitest the praises of Israel. (Psalm 22:3)

The fear of the LORD is the beginning of wisdom: and the knowledge of the holy is understanding. (Proverbs 9:10)

And one cried unto another, and said, Holy, holy, holy, is the LORD of hosts: the whole earth is full of his glory. (Isaiah 6:3)

They say that when Leonardo DaVinci painted his famous *Last Supper* he had little difficulty with any of it except the faces.

Then he painted the faces in without too much trouble except one. He did not feel himself worthy to paint the face of Jesus. He held off and kept holding off, unwilling to approach it but knowing he must. Then in the impulsive carelessness of despair, he just painted it quickly and let it go. "There is no use," he said. "I can't paint Him."

I feel very much the same way about explaining the holiness of God. I think that same sense of despair is on my heart. There isn't any use for anybody to try to explain holiness. The greatest speakers on this subject can play their oratorical harps, but it sounds tinny and unreal, and when they are through you've listened to music but you haven't seen God.

We Cannot Understand Holiness

I suppose the hardest thing about God to comprehend intellectually is His infinitude. But you can talk about the infinitude of God and not feel yourself a worm. But when you talk about the holiness of God, you have not only the problem of an intellectual grasp, but also a sense of personal vileness, which is almost too much to bear.

The reason for this is that we are fallen beings—spiritually, morally, mentally and physically. We are fallen in all the ways that man can fall. Each one of us is born into a tainted world, and we learn impurity from our cradles. We nurse it in with our mother's milk, we breathe it in the very air. Our education deepens it and our experience confirms it—evil impurities everywhere. Everything is dirty; even our whitest white is dingy gray.

Our noblest heroes are soiled heros, all of them. So we learn to excuse and to overlook and not to expect too much. We don't expect all truth from our teachers, and we don't expect faithfulness from our politicians. We quickly forgive them when they lie to us and vote for them again. We don't expect honesty from our merchants. We don't expect complete trustworthiness from anybody. And we manage to get along in the world only by passing laws to protect ourselves not only from the criminal element but from the best people there are who might in the moment of temptation take advantage of us.

This kind of world gets into our pores, into our nerves, until we have lost the ability to conceive of the holy. Still, I will endeavor to discuss the holiness of God, the Holy One. We cannot comprehend it, and we certainly cannot define it.

Holiness means purity, but "purity" doesn't describe it well enough. Purity merely means that it is unmixed, with nothing else in it. But that isn't enough. We talk of moral excellency, but that isn't adequate. To be morally excellent is to exceed someone else in moral character. But when we say that God is morally excellent, who is it that He exceeds? The angels, the seraphim? Surely He does—but that still isn't enough. We mean rectitude; we mean honor; we mean truth and righteousness; we mean all of these—uncreated and eternal.

God is not now any holier than He ever was. For He, being unchanging and unchangeable, can never become holier than He is. And He never was holier than He is, and He'll never be any holier than now. His moral excellence implies self-existence, for He did not get His holiness from anyone nor from anywhere. He did not go off into some vast, infinitely distant realm and there absorb His holiness; He is Himself the Holiness. He is the All-Holy, the Holy One; He is holiness itself, beyond the power of thought to grasp or of word to express, beyond the power of all praise.

Language cannot express the holy, so God resorts to association and suggestion. He cannot say it outright because He would have to use words for which we know no meaning. He would have to translate it down into our unholiness. If He were to tell us how white He is, we would understand it in terms of only dingy gray.

God cannot tell us by language, so He uses association and suggestion and shows how holiness affects the unholy. He shows Moses at the burning bush before the holy, fiery Presence, kneeling down to take his shoes from his feet, hiding his face, for he was afraid to look upon God.

> And the LORD said unto Moses, Lo, I come unto thee in a thick cloud, that the people may hear when I speak with thee, and believe thee for ever. And Moses told the words of the people unto the LORD. And the LORD said unto Moses, Go unto the people,

and sanctify them to day and to morrow, and
let them wash their clothes, and be ready
against the third day: for the third day the
LORD will come down in the sight of all the
people upon mount Sinai. And thou shalt set
bounds unto the people round about, saying,
Take heed to yourselves, that ye go not up
into the mount, or touch the border of it:
whosoever toucheth the mount shall be
surely put to death: There shall not an hand
touch it, but he shall surely be stoned, or
shot through; whether it be beast or man, it
shall not live: when the trumpet soundeth
long, they shall come up to the mount. And
Moses went down from the mount unto the
people, and sanctified the people; and they
washed their clothes.
(Exodus 19:9-14)

Moses did the best he could. He went down and
tried to clean up their dingy gray.

And it came to pass on the third day in
the morning, that there were thunders and
lightnings, and a thick cloud upon the
mount, and the voice of the trumpet ex-
ceeding loud; so that all the people that was
in the camp trembled. And Moses brought
forth the people out of the camp to meet
with God; and they stood at the nether part
of the mount. And mount Sinai was altogether on a smoke, because the LORD de-

scended upon it in fire: and the smoke thereof ascended as the smoke of a furnace, and the whole mount quaked greatly. And when the voice of the trumpet sounded long, and waxed louder and louder, Moses spake, and God answered him by a voice. And the LORD came down upon mount Sinai, on the top of the mount: and the LORD called Moses up to the top of the mount; and Moses went up. And the LORD said unto Moses, Go down, charge the people, lest they break through unto the LORD to gaze, and many of them perish. (19:16-21)

All the trumpeting and the voice and the fire and smoke and shaking of the mount—this was God saying by suggestion and association what we couldn't understand in words.

Two Words for Holiness

There are two particular words for holy in the Hebrew Bible. One word is used almost exclusively of God the Holy One and rarely used of anything or person except God the Holy One. In Proverbs 9:10 it says, "The fear of the LORD is the beginning of wisdom: and the knowledge of the holy is understanding." I am greatly fascinated by the fact that the King James Bible refers to it in the abstract—"the holy" rather than "the Holy One." And yet the Jewish Bible says "the knowledge of the Holy One."

Proverbs 30:3 also uses this phrase: "I neither

learned wisdom, nor have *the knowledge of the holy.*" Again, the Jewish Bible translates it "the knowledge of the Holy One" or "the All-Holy." The Jewish translators encountered exactly the same word more than forty times and translated it "the Holy One." So obviously this is God! And yet there is enough vagueness about it that the King James translators felt free to make it abstract and call it "the holy."

There is another word for "holy" that is not used of God very often. It is not as "high" a word; it is used often of created things. It is something that is "holy by contact or association" with something holy. We hear of holy ground or holy Sabbath or holy city or holy people or holy works. It's not the same awesome, awe-filled word that He uses when He says "the holy" or "the Holy One."

In the New Testament, we have a Greek word about God being holy. "Be ye holy; for I am holy" (1 Peter 1:16). I notice that the definition of that Greek word is "Awful [full of awe] Thing." Now think of that. *The Awful Thing*—that's one meaning of the word holy—the Holy One!

Let's think a little about the Holy One and His creatures. We see that this Holy One allows only holy beings into His Presence. Yet in our humanistic day—our day of a watered-down, sentimental Christianity that blows its nose loudly and makes God into a poor, weak, weeping old man—in this awful day, that sense of the holy isn't upon the Church.

I hear of a lot of people doing specialized minis-

tries these days. If we're going to be specialized
then I think we ought to specialize on the right
thing. And therefore if I'm going to emphasize God
and the holiness of God and the awful, unapproachable quality that can be called "that Awful
Thing," I think I'm on the right track. It hasn't
completely disappeared, but it's something we've
almost lost in our day. We have lost the sense of
the Holy One almost altogether.

> And all the angels stood round about the
> throne, and about the elders and the four
> beasts, and fell before the throne on their
> faces, and worshipped God, saying, Amen:
> Blessing, and glory, and wisdom, and
> thanksgiving, and honour, and power, and
> might, be unto our God for ever and ever.
> Amen. And one of the elders answered, say-
> ing unto me, What are these which are ar-
> rayed in white robes? and whence came
> they? And I said unto him, Sir, thou
> knowest. And he said to me, These are they
> which came out of great tribulation, and
> have washed their robes, and made them
> white in the blood of the Lamb. Therefore
> are they before the throne of God, and serve
> him day and night in his temple: and he that
> sitteth on the throne shall dwell among
> them. (Revelation 7:11-15)

There are people in the presence of God, but
they're there only by a technical redemption. I

worry in this hour that we're "technically" Christians. We can prove that we are—but anybody can flip open a Greek lexicon and show you that you are a saint. But I'm afraid of that kind of Christianity. If I haven't felt the sense of vileness by contrast with that sense of unapproachable and indescribable holiness, I wonder if I have ever been hit hard enough to really repent. And if I don't repent, I wonder if I can believe.

Nowadays we're given a quick fix and we're told just to believe it, and then we give our names and addresses and we're all right. But I'm afraid our fathers knew God in a different manner than that. James Ussher, the seventeenth-century Irish archbishop, used to go out to the riverbank, kneel down by a log and repent of his sins all Saturday afternoon—though there probably wasn't a holier man in all the region. He felt how unutterably vile he was; he couldn't stand the dingy gray which was the whitest thing he had set over against the unapproachable shining whiteness that was God.

The Fiery Holiness of God

Go to the book of Isaiah: "Above [the throne] stood the seraphims: each one had six wings; with twain he covered his face, and with twain he covered his feet, and with twain he did fly" (6:2). There wasn't any of the flippancy that we see now. There wasn't any tendency to try to be funnier than a clown. There was a sense of Presence, and the holy creatures covered their feet. Why? They covered their feet in modesty, and they covered their face in worship, and they used their other wings to fly. These were the seraphim; they're called "fiery burners." Then there is Ezekiel, chapter 1, where the creatures come out of a fire.

God speaks of Himself often as fire. "Our God is a consuming fire," it says in Hebrews 12:29. And in Isaiah 33:14: "Who among us shall dwell with the devouring fire? who among us shall dwell with everlasting burnings?"

People sometimes use this text to ask, "Who of you is going to go to hell?" but if you will read it in its context this does not describe hell. Almost all commentators agree on this, because the next verse says that it is "He that walketh righteously, and speaketh uprightly; he that despiseth the gain of oppressions, that shaketh his hands from holding of bribes, that stoppeth his ears from hearing of blood, and shutteth his eyes from seeing evil" (33:15).

What is this devouring fire? It is not hell, but the presence of God. Who among us shall dwell in the fiery burnings? Do you not know that fire can dwell with fire? You can put the iron into the fire and the iron can learn to live with the fire by absorbing the fire and beginning to glow in incandescent brightness in the fire. So we will dwell in the fire; these creatures in Ezekiel came out of the fire, and they let down their wings to worship. At the Word of God's command they leap to do His will, these awesome holy creatures about which we know so little and about which we ought to know more.

God showed Himself as fire when He spoke to Moses out of the burning bush (Exodus 3:2). He went with them in the pillar of fire:

> And the LORD went before them by day in a pillar of a cloud, to lead them the way; and by night in a pillar of fire, to give them light; to go by day and night: He took not away the pillar of the cloud by day, nor the pillar of fire by night, from before the people. (Exodus 13:21-22)

God was dwelling there in that awesome fire. Then when the tabernacle was made and the cherubim of gold overshadowed the mercy seat, what was it that came down between the cherubim wings? What was it that only one man could see, and he only once a year with blood? I wonder how many high priests ever looked at the Shekinah, with all of the protection of the atoning blood and the commandment of God. The priest would go through the great, heavy veil that took four men to part it. And this man went in trembling into the Presence.

I wonder if, being Jewish and worshiping the great God Almighty, the Holy One of Israel, one in twenty ever dared gaze on that fire. He was not told he couldn't, but I wonder if anybody ever dared do it. I notice that the very seraphim covered their faces. Moses "hid his face; for he was afraid to look upon God" (Exodus 3:6). John fell down when he saw the Savior and had to be raised up again almost from the dead (Revelation 1:17).

Every encounter with God has been such that man went flat down and went blind. Paul went blind on the Damascus road (see Acts 9). What was the light that blinded him? Was it a cosmic ray coming down from some exploding body or from two colliding galaxies? No! It was the God of Abraham, Isaac and Jacob, the God that dwelt in the bush, the God that dwelt in the Shekinah between the wings of the seraphim.

When they were all together in one place and suddenly there came a sound from heaven as the rushing of a mighty wind and fire appeared and sat as a tongue of flame upon each one of them (see Acts 2:1-3)—what was it? What could it mean but that God was branding them on their foreheads with His fiery holiness to say, "You're mine now"?

The Church was born out of fire, just as the creatures in Ezekiel 1 came out of fire. We have gray ashes today, but we are to be men and women of fire, for that is our origin.

Here are the words that tell us how God shall some day untomb the sky:

> But the heavens and the earth, which are now, by the same word are kept in store, reserved unto fire against the day of judgment. . . . [T]he heavens shall pass away with a great noise, and the elements shall melt with fervent heat. . . . [T]he heavens

being on fire shall be dissolved. . . . (2 Peter
3:7, 10, 12)

What is that fire? Is it to be the atomic fire of a
hydrogen bomb? Don't allow yourself to be fooled
by the scientists. Don't let your spiritual concepts
and perceptions be dragged down to a research
laboratory. That awesome fire out of which the
seraphim moved, that fire that dwelt between the
cherubim and that blazing light that knocked Paul
flat—that's the same fire that shall dissolve the
heaven and the earth: the awful presence of that
Holy Thing, that Awful Thing. (Don't be offended
because I say *Thing*—I know He is a Person, God
the Holy One of Israel. But there is something
about Him that is awesome and awful.)

The Holy One and the Sinner

This Holy One confronts the sinner, who
thinks he is going to decide when he'll serve
Christ. He is going to push God around. He is going to decide whether to accept Jesus or not, receive Him or not, obey Him or not. He is going to
go proudly down the aisle with his chest out.

The sinner—who will lay his head on his pillow
tonight with a heartbeat between him and eternity—tells himself, *I'll decide this question. I'm a man
of free will. God isn't forcing my will.* No, He
won't—but I have words for the sinner. "Art thou
not from everlasting, O LORD my God, mine Holy
One? . . . Thou art of purer eyes than to behold evil,
and canst not look on iniquity" (Habakkuk 1:12-13).

People say, "Are your problems too much for you? Jesus will handle your problems. Are you troubled mentally? Jesus will give you mental peace. Do you have trouble at the office? Jesus will help you at the office." All this is true—but oh, how far it is from biblical religion! God was in their midst!

What was it that gathered the people together in the book of Acts? They ministered unto the Lord and fasted and prayed. And there in the awesome presence they heard the voice of the Holy Spirit say, "Separate me Barnabas and Saul" (Acts 13:2). Now when the church gathers, we're thrown back on our planning, our reasoning and our thinking—when the great and holy God is in our midst.

I would recommend that you remember these words: "Thou art of purer eyes than to behold evil." You have evil in your life, your heart, your home, your business, your memory—all unconfessed, unforgiven and uncleansed. Remember that it is only by the infinite patience of God that you are not consumed (see Lamentations 3:22). "Our God is a consuming fire" (Hebrews 12:29). And it is also written, "Follow . . . holiness, without which no man shall see the Lord" (12:14). Teachers come from everywhere with their dingy gray interpretations, pulling this down and explaining it away and saying, "See note on such and such." But it stands—"holiness, without which no man shall see the Lord."

If you can interpret that neatly and go home without being bothered, I wonder if your eyes have ever gazed upon that Awful Thing. I wonder if you have "the knowledge of the holy" (Proverbs 9:10). I wonder if that sense of the overwhelming, crushing holiness of God has ever come upon your heart.

It was a common thing in other days, when God was the center of human worship, to kneel at an altar and shake, tremble, weep and perspire in an agony of conviction. They expected it in that day. We don't see it now because the God we preach is not the everlasting, awful God, "mine Holy One," who is "of purer eyes than to behold evil, and canst not look on iniquity."

We've used the technical interpretation of justification by faith and the imputed righteousness of Christ until we've watered down the wine of our spirituality. God help us in this evil hour!

We come into the presence of God with tainted souls. We come with our own concept of morality, having learned it from books, from the newspaper and from school. We come to God dirty—our whitest white is dirty, our churches are dirty and our thoughts are dirty—and do nothing about it!

If we came to God dirty, but trembling and shocked and awestruck in His presence, if we knelt at His feet and cried with Isaiah, "I am undone; because I am a man of unclean lips" (Isaiah 6:5), then I could understand. But we skip into His awful presence. We're dirty, but we have a book called *Seven Steps to Salvation* that gives us seven verses to get us out of our problems. And each year we have more Christians, more people going to church, more church buildings, more money—and less spirituality and less holiness. We're forgetting "holiness, without which no man shall see the Lord."

I tell you this: I want God to be what God is: the impeccably holy, unapproachable Holy Thing, the All-Holy One. I want Him to be and remain *THE HOLY*. I want His heaven to be holy and His throne to be holy. I don't want Him to change or modify His requirements. Even if it shuts me out, I want something holy left in the universe.

You can join almost any church now. I've heard recently of a certain church where at the closing hymn they open the doors and anybody can join. A *gangster* can join. I say, "Never, never, never!" If they can't get into heaven, they ought not get into our churches! We let our churches stay dingy gray instead of pleading for holy whiteness.

As soon as anybody begins to plead for Christians to be holy, somebody comes along and says, "Now, brother, don't get excited about this; don't become a fanatic. God understands our flesh; He knows that we are but dust." He knows we are but dust, but He also says He is "of purer eyes than to behold evil, and canst not look on iniquity" and that without holiness, "no man shall see the Lord."

Thomas Binney wrote one of the most awesome, wondrous things ever written:

Eternal Light! Eternal Light!
How pure the soul must be

When, placed within Thy searching sight,
It shrinks not, but with calm delight
   Can live and look on Thee.

The spirits that surround Thy throne
   May bear the burning bliss;
But that is surely theirs alone,
Since they have never, never known
   A fallen world like this.

Oh, how shall I, whose native sphere
   Is dark, whose mind is dim,
Before th'Ineffable appear,
And on my natural spirit bear
   The uncreated beam?

"How shall . . . my natural spirit bear the
uncreated beam"—that fiery beam, out of which
come the "holy burners" who sing, "Holy, holy
holy is the Lord God Almighty"? How can I bear it?
   All your religious helps, all your marked Bibles,
all your jolly, joke-telling, banqueting Christian
friends—all of these will mean nothing when each
one of us is called "before the Ineffable [to] appear and on our naked spirits bear the uncreated
beam." How are we going to do it?

There is a way for man to rise
   To Thee, sublime Abode;
An Offering and a Sacrifice,
A Holy Spirit's energies,
An Advocate with God:

These, these prepare us for the sight
    Of holiness above;
The sons of ignorance and night
May dwell in the eternal Light,
    Through the eternal Love.

I think that's one of the greatest things ever written by mortal man. We don't sing it much; it is too awful and we're afraid of it.

"The spirits that surround Thy throne"—the seraphim, cherubim, angels, archangels, principalities, powers, unfallen creatures—"can bear the burning bliss," but that's because "they have never, never known a fallen world like this."

But how can I "bear the burning bliss"? It isn't enough for somebody to mark a New Testament and rub my nose in it and try to comfort me. *I don't want to be comforted!* I want to know what it will be like in that hour when I leave my wife, my children, my grandchildren and all my good friends. There's not one of them that can help me in that awful hour when I appear before the Ineffable, and the uncreated beam impinges on my naked spirit.

There is a way. It is through the "offering and the sacrifice" of "the Advocate with God." But don't take that lightly. Conversion used to be a revolutionary, radical, wondrous, terrible, glorious thing. But there's not much of it left. We've forgotten that God is the Holy One of Israel.

Oh God, time is running, flying like a frightened bird. The bird of time is on the wing and has a little way to flutter. The wine of life is oozing drop by drop, and the leaves of life are falling one by one. Soon, before the Ineffable every man must appear to give an account for the deeds done in the body. Oh, Father, keep upon us a sense of holiness that we can't sin and excuse it, but that repentance will be as deep as our lives. This we ask in Christ's name. Amen.

Chapter 10

God's Perfection

Out of Zion, the perfection of beauty, God hath shined. (Psalm 50:2)

In this verse we have three words in special relation to each other—"perfection," "beauty" and "God." And while it is Zion that is called the perfection of beauty, it is the perfection of beauty because God shined out of her.

In trying to understand today's Christianity (and by that I do not mean liberalism or modernism, I mean evangelicalism or gospel Christianity), we must take into account two things which have happened over the last fifty years. We must take into account the gains we have made and the losses we have suffered.

Our Gains and Losses

That the churches have made some gains in the last fifty years cannot be denied by anyone who wants to be truthful. For instance, a higher percentage of the total population go to church than used to, and there are larger numbers of people calling themselves Christians. And then there are multiplying theological schools, seminaries, Bible schools, Christian colleges of various sorts. There is an ever-swelling flood of Christian literature which is being published and spread abroad.

Then there is the popularity of religion in our time. I suppose it is easier when things are popular to propagate them than when they are not. And certainly the gospel is quite popular now. We have to our advantage better systems of communication: radio, television (if you like it), telephone and all other modern means of communicating. We have stepped-up transportation that will allow a preacher to preach in Chicago in the morning and in New York in the evening. And we have various evangelizing organizations that have sprung up over the years.

I was thinking that there isn't a single linguistic group, ethnic group or social group anywhere that doesn't have somebody bent on evangelizing it. We have those who want to evangelize the Jews, businessmen, students, those in hospitals, those in jail and everybody, everywhere. We cannot deny that a lot of good is being done and the gospel is being spread around. Those are the gains that we have made, and there are many others.

But we have suffered some losses in the meantime. These losses I want to name before you. We have lost from our gospel Christianity almost altogether what people used to call religious fear. And along with our loss of religious fear came a corresponding flippancy and familiarity toward God that our fathers never knew.

No Awareness of the Eternal

We have lost also an awareness of the invisible and eternal. The world is too much with us so that the invisible and the eternal seem to be quite forgotten or at least we are not aware of it. We're only briefly aware of it when somebody dies. The Church has lost the consciousness of the divine Presence and the concept of majesty.

I said at a service once that we had so organized our churches that God could leave and we wouldn't find it out. During the week I received a call from a lady who had been at that service, but attends a different gospel church. She was not critical nor harsh but seemed to be brokenhearted. She said, "Mr. Tozer, I heard what you said, that God could leave a church and we would not find it out. I would like to tell you that God has left our church."

I didn't want to be guilty of speaking against the church or of helping her in her criticism of the church, so I said, "Perhaps the Spirit is grieved in your church."

"Oh, it's long past that," she said. "It is long past the Spirit's being grieved. God the Spirit has withdrawn."

Now I don't know how true her judgment was

about it. She was very kind and tender. She was not criticizing so much as simply stating what she believed to be a fact. The consciousness of the divine Presence seems to have left the churches to a very terrible degree.

We also seem to have gotten away from the concept of majesty altogether. This is the age of the common man and along with the common man has come the common god. We have no heroes anymore, because everybody is equal to everybody else, and the common man is now in control. But along with the common man, I say, is the common god, and with it the loss of the whole concept of majesty.

But you say, "Mr. Tozer, isn't there a concept of majesty left? Didn't the whole world carry on when the queen was crowned a few years ago?"[1] That circus that they had on television had no sense of majesty at all in it. There was no majesty there. We have crowned pumpkin queens and cotton queens and other kind of queens in this country, and it was the same mixture of showmanship and sex that is found every place. If that girl had been a homely old lady there wouldn't have been much done. But she was a beautiful young lady and so we had a big time, but majesty was missing. They can say, "Your Majesty," but they don't feel it.

---

1   The coronation of Elizabeth II, Queen of England, occured in 1952.

The modern Christian has lost a sense of worship along with the concept of majesty, and of course, reverence as well. He has lost his ability to withdraw inwardly and commune in the secret place with God in the shrine of his own hidden spirit. It is this that makes Christianity, and we have all but lost it. Added numbers, yes, but lost fear. Multiplied schools, yes, but lost awareness of the invisible. Tons of literature being poured out, of course, but no consciousness of the divine Presence. Better communication, certainly, but nothing to communicate. Evangelistic organizations, yes, but the concept of majesty and worship and reverence has almost left us.

External Gains, Internal Losses

The total result has been that our gains have been external and our losses internal. This is the great tragedy of the hour. And at last our gains may prove to be no more than losses spread over a larger area. Anybody can see that if the quality of our religion is impaired while we are nevertheless extending it to more people, we are losing instead of gaining. If we have only so much glory and we spread it thin, we have not gained anything. I believe that that is where we are. And I believe that we never can recover our glory until we are brought to see again the awful perfections of God.

My conviction has been growing for years that we must recapture the concept of the perfections of God. We must see again how awful [awe-full] God is, how beautiful and how perfect. And we must begin to preach it, sing it, write about it, promote it, talk it, tell it and pray it until we have recaptured the concept of majesty, until the awareness of the divine is back in our religion again, until we have regained the ability and desire to retire within our own hearts and worship God in the silence of our own spirits.

I have tried to turn people from the externals to the internals of religion. I have tried to take away the clouds and show God in His glory. I have stood almost alone in preaching this, and it has been a strange thing. It is rare to hear a man preach anything about God the Holy One. People like to hear about it, and they invite me here and there to preach on it. But why don't we get hold of this idea? I don't know why, but I'm not discouraged.

If we continue as we are, spreading our impaired religion, our weakened Christianity, over a wider area until the Lord comes, the Lord will break through the clouds and will show Himself majestic and wonderful in heaven above and earth beneath and under the sea, and everywhere they shall bow and own Him as Lord and King. But I'd like to see it brought back to the Church before that dramatic hour comes. I'd like to see us know it now.

What Is Perfection?

What does perfection mean? According to Webster, perfection means "the highest possible degree of excellence." That which is perfect lacks nothing it should have and has nothing it should not have. Perfection is fullness and completeness. Something that is perfect is not lacking in anything and doesn't have anything it shouldn't have.

This word "perfection" or "perfect" is a relative word. It's found in the Bible quite a little, because it is the English translation of a number of Hebrew and Greek words. It means "that which is excellent, which is the highest possible degree of excellence." Of course it's a relative word and we use it in various ways. We talk about this or that earthly thing being perfect; the Bible does the same thing.

Perfection is to be complete in your nature. That is, it is to be perfect as it touches you. If something else of another nature were to be like you, it would be imperfect. Let me illustrate this. When a new baby is born, one of the first things the doctor does and one of the first things the anxious mother does is to look him over and see if he's all right. We look for two legs, two arms, two eyes, two ears, one nose. And when we find that everything is the right number and in the right place we smile and say, "Well, thank God for a healthy little baby." That's perfection to a human child.

But suppose that on the farm a little colt is born and is looked over by the anxious farmer. He doesn't look for two legs, he looks for four. And if the thing had only two it would be deformed. If the baby had four legs, it would be deformed. Perfection is having just what it should have, being what it is. Perfection in that relative way would mean a completeness and fullness of what you are.

But we can't think of God like this. If perfection means the highest possible degree of excellence, then we cannot apply this thought to God at all. How can we apply "the highest possible" to God? Is there anything that *isn't* possible with God? As though God had been created and had done the highest thing possible, that He was as perfect as it was possible for Him to be? No, you can't apply that to God; that's only applied to creatures.

No Degrees in God

When I was explaining the infinitude of God I pointed out that there are no degrees in God. God is not at the top of the heap in an ever-ascending perfection of being, from the worm on up until finally we reach God. On the contrary, God is completely different and separate, so that there are no degrees in God. God is simply God, an infinite perfection of fullness, and we cannot say God is a little more or a little less. "More" and "less" are creature-words. We can say that a man has a little more strength today than yesterday. We can say the child is a little taller this year; he's growing. But you can't apply more or less to God, for God is the perfect One; He's just God.

Sometimes when we speak of perfection we use the word *excellence*. Did you ever stop to think what that word means? It means "being in a state of excelling," which implies a *comparison* to something or somebody. Excellence in a musician means that he is a better musician than the other musicians. If he has a high degree of excellence, we could say he has perfection in his field. He doesn't, but we could use the word.

But when you come to God, He says, "To whom then will ye liken me, or shall I be equal?" (Isaiah 40:25). You don't compare God. We say that God is *incomparable*, and by that we mean that God stands alone as God, that nothing can be compared with Him. Isaiah was very strong here, and he wrote some very beautiful and eloquent language, telling us that we must not compare God with anything or anybody—anything in heaven above or on the earth beneath.

Moses' law said, "Thou shalt not make unto thee any graven image, or any likeness of any thing that is in heaven above, or that is in the earth beneath, or that is in the water under the earth" (Exodus 20:4). People thought that meant that you should never make any works of art. But the fact is there were works of art in the temple commanded by God. So God was not against works of art; He was against substituting them for God or thinking they were like God.

"To whom then will ye liken me?" said God. And yet the Bible uses this word *perfect* all the way through, and applies it to God and to things that aren't God. For instance, there is the Lord's command, "Be ye therefore perfect, even as your Father which is in heaven is perfect" (Matthew 5:48). In the original Greek, exactly the same word that applies to God applies to people, too.

Do you know why God uses the same word? Because there isn't any other word. You cannot find the language that will tell what God is. So God does the best He can, considering who and what we are, to make Himself known to us. God is not limited in Himself. He is limited in us. Paul said, "ye are straitened in your own [hearts]" (2 Corinthians 6:12), which means "It's yourself—you're narrowed in your own hearts." The inability of God to get through to us is not due to the imperfection of the Great God, but the imperfection of the man to whom He is trying to give the truth.

When we apply perfection to God, we mean that He has unqualified fullness and completeness of whatever He has. He has unqualified plenitude of power. He also has unqualified fullness of wisdom. He has unqualified knowledge. He has unqualified holiness.

When I say that a man is a perfect singer, I qualify that in my mind. I think, *Well, he does the best a person can.* But when I say that God is holy, I do not qualify it. I mean it fully and completely. God is what He is and that's it. God's power and being, His wisdom and knowledge, His holiness and goodness, His justice and mercy, His love and grace—all of these and more of the attributes of God—are in shining, full, uncreated perfection. They are called the beauty of the Lord our God.

"And let the beauty of the LORD our God be upon us," Moses said in Psalm 90:17, and David said, "One thing have I desired of the LORD, that will I seek after; that I may dwell in the house of the LORD all the days of my life, to behold the beauty of the LORD, and to inquire in his temple" (27:4). "The beauty of the LORD" means that God has all He should have of everything, a fullness of everything. If it is love, then there is no limit to the love of God. If it is mercy, then there is no limit to the mercy of God. If it is grace, there are no bounds to the grace of God. If it is goodness, there is no limit to the goodness of God. And this is called the beauty of the Lord our God.

"Out of Zion, the perfection of beauty, God hath shined" (Psalm 50:2). Why was Zion the earthly perfection of beauty? Because her beauty came from the shining God who dwelt between the wings of the cherubim. She was not only architecturally beautiful but all the concepts of her were beautiful. Her hymnody was beautiful. Her ideas of worship were beautiful, shining there in the sun, knowing that God was there between the wings of the cherubim dwelling in the *shekinah*.[2] She was beautiful above all the earth. All things as they move toward God are beautiful. And they are ugly as they move away from Him.

What Honors God Is Beautiful

The older I get the more I love hymns, and the

---

2   A Hebrew term applied to the visible manifestation of God's presence.

less I love secular music. Secular music, however beautiful and artistic it may be and however it may express the genius of the composer, has one jewel missing from its crown. But a hymn, though it may not reflect the same degree of genius and a good musician might find fault with it, is still beautiful because it has God there. The song that honors God is bound to be beautiful.

That's why Psalm 23 is so beautiful—because it honors God. And so it is with the whole Bible itself; it is a shining, beautiful book. It is lovely, whether bound in the cheapest paper or the most expensive leather, whether printed on newsprint or the finest India paper. It is a beautiful book.

Theology itself is a beautiful thing, beautiful because it is the mind reasoning about God. It is the mind down on its knees in a state of breathless devotion, reasoning about God—or it should be. It is possible for theology to become a very hard and aloof thing, and we can lose God right out of our theology. But the kind of theology I'm talking about, the study of God, is a beautiful thing.

That's why I suppose as a man gets older he goes to David more and to Plato less. That's why he goes to Aristotle less and to Paul more. There is beauty in Paul and David, for Paul and David celebrated the perfection of God, while the others dealt with other matters altogether.

Heaven is the place of supreme beauty. I think we ought to rethink our whole concept of heaven; we ought to begin to pray and to search the Scriptures about it. If you were going to Paris you would at least look at a brochure to know where you were going. And if you are going to heaven I think you ought to know something about it.

There's a lot told about it in the Scriptures, but we're so busy living down here that we're not too concerned about it. I'm not going to try to describe it; I'm afraid that the mind of anyone who attempted to describe heaven would go bad on him for very heaviness. It cannot be done. But heaven is the place of supreme beauty, that much we can say. And why? Because the perfection of beauty is there.

"Let the beauty of the LORD our God be upon us" (Psalm 90:17). Was there ever anything more beautiful than the story of Jesus' birth? Was there ever anything more beautiful than the picture of Jesus walking up and down among men in tenderness of humility, healing the sick and raising the dead, forgiving sinners and restoring poor fallen people back to society again? Is there anything more wonderful than His going out to the cross to die for those who were crucifying Him?

Was there anything lovelier than to be the Creator of His own mother, to have made the very body that gave Him protection and bore Him at last into the world? Was anything more awful and awesome and mysterious than that God-Man walking about among men, saying, "I beheld Satan as lightning fall from heaven" (Luke 10:18) and "Before Abraham was, I am" (John 8:58)? He was "the only begotten Son, which is in the bosom of the Father" (John 1:18).

Beauty Centers around Christ

All beauty centers around Jesus Christ. That is why, apart from the commercialism, Christmas is such a beautiful thing. And that is why Easter is so beautiful. To me, Easter is more beautiful than Christmas because Easter celebrates a triumph, and Christmas celebrates the coming of Someone who hadn't yet fought. He had been born to fight, but He hadn't fought. But when Easter comes, we sing, "The three sad days are quickly sped; He rises glorious from the dead."[3] And there's beauty there, though not the beauty of color, outline or physical proportion. You can worship Him in a stable; you can worship Him in a coal mine; you can worship Him in a factory.

It's not the external beauty that is beautiful but the internal beauty. Heaven is beautiful because it is the expression of that which is the perfection of beauty. And while that is true of heaven, I must also say that hell is the place of unrelieved, monstrous ugliness, because there is no perfection; there is only monstrous moral deformity. There is nothing beautiful in hell. And in heaven, of course, there is supreme beauty.

Earth lies halfway between. Earth knows ugli-

---

3   \'93The Strife Is O'er,\'94 translated by Francis Pott.

ness and beauty; it's halfway between heaven and
hell. And the inhabitants of earth must decide
whether they are to seek the beauty of heaven or
the monstrous, unrelieved ugliness of hell.

People worry about whether there is fire in hell
or not. I have no reason not to believe it; what the
Bible says I take as the truth. I would not hesitate to
refer to the fires of hell, for the Scripture talks about
the "lake of fire" (Revelation 20:14-15). But if there
were no fire in hell, if hell were a habitable country,
it still would be the ugliest country in the universe,
the most shockingly deformed place that is known
in the creation because there is none of the perfection of beauty. Only God is absolutely perfect.

Nothing Bad Is Beautiful

It is not possible for anything bad to be beautiful. The Scripture says that we're to "worship the
LORD in the beauty of holiness" (Psalm 29:2). It
is possible for an unholy thing to be pretty or attractive, even charming. But it is not possible for
it to be beautiful. Only that which is holy can be
beautiful ultimately.

"Worship the LORD," says the Scripture, "in
the beauty of holiness." That's no casual remark,
no casual relation of word to word—the beauty of
holiness and the perfection of beauty, and the fact
that only God is perfect. They all fit in together
beautifully and drop into place, for God is beautiful beyond all description. "How beautiful the
sight of God must be," says the hymn. And how
unutterably ugly the sight of hell must be.

If you could think of a prison, if you could think of a place where all hope and mercy had fled, then you would be thinking of hell. If you could think of a place where all moral wisdom was absent, all holiness gone and all goodness absent, where there was no justice, mercy, love, kindness, grace, tenderness or charity, but only multiplied monstrous fullness of unholiness, moral folly, hate, cruelty and injustice—then you would think of hell. This is why God calls us to Himself.

When are we going to raise up a crop of preachers who will begin to preach the perfection of God and tell the people what they ought to hear—that Jesus Christ was born of the Virgin Mary and suffered under Pontius Pilate to die and rise again? He rose that He might save us from the everlasting monstrosities, the uglinesses that are far from God, that are not God. He will bring us to the beauty that is God. He came to call us away from all evil, away from the deformity and eternal ugliness which is hell, and toward holiness, perfection and eternal beauty.

Jesus Christ is God come to us, for "God was in Christ, reconciling the world unto himself " (2 Corinthians 5:19). Oh, how beautiful is the thought that God came to us in that lowly manger bed! How beautiful that He came to us and walked among us! He came with our shape and form, bearing on Himself our humanity, that He might cleanse, purify, purge, remake and restore us, in order to take us back with Him again to that place which is the perfection of beauty.

I don't know where heaven is. I read that the people in the space program shot a gold-plated arrow sixty-some thousand miles into the air, and some are wondering if it might not be reaching heaven at last. I have to smile at that, because God does not dwell in space; space is nothing to God. The great infinite heart of God gathers up into Himself all space.

Our space program is like a baby playing with a rubber ball in Wrigley Field. He can't do anything but bat it around and crawl after it. If he bats it away two feet, he squeals with delight as if he hit a home run. But way out there, 400 feet long, stretches the field. It takes a strong man to knock a ball over the fence.

When man sends up his little arrow, and it reaches the moon and goes into orbit round it, he boasts about it for years to come. Go on, little boy, play with your rubber ball. But the great God who carries the universe in His heart smiles. He is not impressed. He is calling mankind to Himself, to His holiness, beauty, love, mercy and goodness. He has come to reconcile us and call us back.

Nothing Wonderful in the World

I ask you, what has the world to offer? Nothing. We are being bombarded constantly by advertisers who are trying to make us believe that the gadgets they manufacture are worthy of our attention. No, if you want to go someplace and you need a car, get one, but don't imagine it's wonderful. If you want to fly to San Francisco, fly, but don't imagine it's wonderful. Don't imagine anything is wonderful.

"His name shall be called Wonderful" (Isaiah 9:6), and only He can engage and excite the wonder of angels and seraphim and cherubim and archangels and all beings and creatures. Only He is wonderful, and He came to us to reconcile us unto Himself. How beautiful, how wonderful!

There is a song that says, "Take all my mortal interests and let them die, and give me only God." If you want to pray strategically, in a way which would please God, pray that God might raise up men who would see the beauty of the Lord our God and would begin to preach it and hold it out to people, instead of offering peace of mind, deliverance from cigarettes, a better job and a nicer cottage.

God does deliver men from cigarettes; He does help businessmen; He does answer prayer. But they are only incidentals. They're the kindergarten stage of religion. Why can't we go on beyond it and say with the psalmist, "Out of Zion, the perfection of beauty, God hath shined" (Psalm 50:2), and look on the hilltop and see the city of our God, the new Jerusalem? God, the Wonder of the universe, is shining out of it.

What good is all our busy religion if God isn't in it? What good is it if we've lost majesty, reverence, worship—an awareness of the divine? What good is it if we've lost a sense of the Presence and the ability to retreat within our own hearts and meet God in the garden? If we've lost that, why build another church? Why make more converts to an effete Christianity? Why bring people to follow after a Savior so far off that He doesn't own them?

We need to improve the quality of our Christianity, and we never will until we raise our concept of God back to that held by apostle, sage, prophet, saint and reformer. When we put God back where He belongs, we will instinctively and automatically move up again; the whole spiral of our religious direction will be upward. But we try to work it out by methods; we try to produce it by technology; we try to create revivals by publicity stunts.

We try to promote religion, forgetting that it rests upon the character of God. If I have a low concept of God, my religion can only be a cheap, watery affair. But if my concept of God is worthy of God then it can be noble and dignified; it can be reverent, profound, beautiful. This is what I want to see once more among men. Pray that way, won't you?

Oh God our Father, how easy it is to backslide, to be living and yet be dead. How easy it is to become part of a troop of jolly church people, chattering and giggling, while the world grows old, the judgment draws near, hell enlarges its borders and the antichrist prepares himself to take over. While the world is unifying itself and getting ready for a king, oh God, my church is playing and saying, "I am rich, and increased with goods, and have need of nothing" (Revelation 3:17). We have more people attending, we have more money than we ever had. Our churches cost more and our schools are full and our programs are many. But we are forgetting, oh my God, that the quality of our Christianity has been greatly impaired.

Oh, restore again, we cry, restore again to Thy Church her vision of Thee. Restore again to Thy Church her sight of the great God. Show us Thy face, Thy lovely face, a permanent view of Majesty. We will not ask for a transient beam; we want a permanent sight of Thee in all Thy wonder.

Oh God, men sin on and on while they smile at religion; they laugh about it and tolerate it. But, oh God, we have lost our fear and our sense of majesty and our awe. Give back to us, we pray, the majesty in the heavens; give back to us a sight of majesty again so we can know how wonderful Thou art. "Thy majesty, how bright; how beautiful Thy mercy seat in depths of burning light."

Send us forth to pray, to walk about knowing that we are in the garden indeed, even as thou didst walk "in the garden in the cool of the day" (Genesis 3:8), and Adam hid. Oh, how many of us, Lord, hide behind one thing or another because we are not morally and spiritually prepared to come out and walk with Thee. But "Enoch walked with God: and he was not; for God took him" (5:24). Moses looked upon Thy face, and his face did shine (see Exodus 34:29). Oh God, send us out not only to make converts, but to glorify the Father and to hold up the beauty of Jesus Christ to men. All this we ask in the name of Jesus Christ our Lord. Amen.

The
ATTRIBUTES
of
GOD

VOLUME 1
STUDY GUIDE

by

DAVID E. FESSENDEN

A.W. TOZER

WingSpread Publishers
Chicago, Illinois

Contents

Acknowledgments

Many people have helped me in this effort, but I especially want to thank:

Jon Graf, who paved the way for Tozer study guides through his *Study Guide for The Pursuit of God*, which I used as a template for this guide.

Dan Boreman and his class at Immanuel Alliance, for dedicating a Sunday school quarter to try out these lessons.

My wife, who bravely gave up many hours together for this.

How to Use This Guide

This study guide has been developed to help you get the most out of A.W. Tozer's *The Attributes of God Volume One*. It should enable you to understand more clearly what Tozer is saying and to apply to your own life the truths he sets forth.

The study guide is designed for both personal and group use. The personal study section (the material that comes first in each session of this guide) should be read after you read the corresponding chapter in *The Attributes of God Volume One*. Let its comments and questions help you reflect on the major points Tozer is making. It will also provide you with additional Scripture to read and study. The group study section offers a lesson plan and discussion questions for those wishing to use *The Attributes of God Volume One* as the text for an adult Sunday school class or a small group study.

Personal Study

Whether you are studying personally or as the leader of a class or small group, you will want to begin by reading the personal study section of session 1. It provides background information on A.W. Tozer and the two volumes of *The Attributes of God*.

1

From that point on, the best method of study will be to read thoughtfully a chapter from *The Attributes of God Volume One* and then follow through with the related study guide lesson. Unless you are a group leader, you need not read the "LESSON PLAN— Group Study" section.

Group Study—Leader's Instructions

As you prepare for each session of your class or group, you will want to read the entire section of this guide that coincides with the chapter of *The Attributes of God Volume One* that your group is studying. In other words, you need to read both the personal study section and the group lesson plans.

The group lesson plans are set up with the same subtitles used for the personal study. This is to help you find information quickly. When the activity recommends that you read a quotation from *The Attributes of God Volume One*, the page numbers from the text of the book are usually provided, or the quotation is in the personal study section of this guide under the correlating subtitle. The personal study section will also suggest to you things of significance that you will wish to stress.

Naturally, *all* members should have a copy of *The Attributes of God Volume One* and keep up with the reading assignments. These lessons, however, are designed so that members who do not keep up with the reading assignments can still get some benefit from the class.

Introduction:
A.W. Tozer and God's Attributes

Personal Study

Supplementary Materials: David J. Fant, Jr., *A.W. Tozer: A Twentieth-Century Prophet* (Camp Hill, PA: WingSpread Publishers, 1964; reprint, 2002); James Snyder, *In Pursuit of God: The Life of A.W. Tozer* (1991); A.W. Tozer, *The Knowledge of the Holy* (San Francisco: Harper and Row, 1961).

Welcome to *The Attributes of God Volume One*. Before you begin the first chapter, it may be helpful to learn a little about the author of this book and about how this volume came to be.

A.W. Tozer was born on a small farm in rural Pennsylvania. He came to Christ as a young man and began the pastoral ministry without any college or seminary training. He served only a few churches in his forty-four years of ministry, thirty-one of those years in a modest congregation in Chicago. Nothing in his background would indicate the profound impact he would have on the lives of millions of believers around the globe.

While he enjoyed a healthy reputation as a preacher, if it were not for his writing ability, he might never have gained the worldwide prominence he did. His two most popular books—*The Pursuit of God* and *The Knowledge of the Holy*—are considered classics in the genres of Christian living and popular theology.

The two volumes of *The Attributes of God* are something of a combination of these two best-sellers, in that they cover the same topic as *The Knowledge of the Holy* (God's attributes) but they have the devotional flavor of *The Pursuit of God*. Each attribute of God that is discussed in these two books is presented in the light of the believer's personal relationship with God.

Both volumes of *The Attributes of God* began as a series of taped messages—which might be a drawback if it were a preacher other than Tozer. The transcripts of most sermons, even many very good ones, can make for dull reading because there is a definite loss in the power of expression when the message moves from the medium of live speech to printed page. Not so with Tozer. It is said that he wrote his sermons in the format of a magazine article, which could explain why they retain so much of their dynamism on paper.

In addition, I have carefully but lightly edited the material to trim out the almost unavoidable redundancies and confusing phraseology inherent in any spoken message. I strove to maintain Tozer's "voice" while smoothing out the text to the high quality of his other written works. The result is a quite readable series of chapters on God's attributes, compiled in a format I think Tozer would have found acceptable.

As you begin this study, one question may come to your mind: Why was Tozer drawn to preach on God's attributes in the first place? The answer to that is wrapped up in the consuming ambition to which he dedicated his life.

Tozer was a man driven by a desire to know God in His fullness. Jon Graf, in his study guide to *The Pursuit of God*, said that Tozer once confessed to his lifelong friend Robert Battles, "I want to love God more than anyone in my generation." Graf goes on to say, "To some of us that may sound selfish and arrogant, but for Tozer it wasn't. It simply came out of an honest desire to enrich his relationship with the Lord."

The desire to know God more deeply and more intimately naturally led Tozer to study God's attributes. As he himself said in this very volume,

> Christianity at any given time is strong or weak depending upon her concept of God. And I insist upon this and I have said it many times, that the basic trouble with the Church today is her unworthy conception of God. (p. 41)

Ponder for a moment these other comments by Tozer about our need to know *about* God if we truly intend to *know* God:

> It is vitally important that we think soundly about God. Since He is the foundation of all our religious beliefs, it follows that if we err in our ideas of God, we will go astray on everything else.
>
> *This World: Playground or Battleground?*

5

The hope of the Church yet lies in the purity of her theology, that is, her beliefs about God and man and their relation to each other.

The Set of the Sail

Often enough we have been warned that the morality of any nation or civilization will follow its concepts of God. A parallel truth is less often heard: When a church begins to think impurely and inadequately about God, decline sets in.

We must think nobly and speak worthily of God. Our God is sovereign. We would do well to follow our old-fashioned forebears who knew what it was to kneel in breathless, wondering adoration in the presence of the God who is willing to claim us as His own through grace.

Jesus, Our Man in Glory

Worship, I say, rises or falls with our concept of God; that is why I do not believe in these half-converted cowboys who call God "the Man Upstairs." I do not think they worship at all because their concept of God is unworthy of God and unworthy of them. And if there is one terrible disease in the Church of Christ, it is that we do not see God as great as He is.

Worship: The Missing Jewel

As you go through this study guide, whether by yourself or as a group, ask yourself these questions:

- How does my understanding of this particular attribute have implications for my relationship with God?
- If I truly understood and believed in this attribute of God, how would it change the way I live?

By keeping these questions in your mind as you read and study, I believe you will get the maximum benefit from *The Attributes of God Volume One*. May the Lord bless you in your journey into the Father's heart.

LESSON PLAN—Group Study

AIM: To help my students prepare for this study of God's attributes by defining what an attribute is and discussing why Tozer chose to preach about them.

Introduction

1. Open with prayer.

2. Have someone read Jeremiah 9:24. Have the group discuss what it means to "understand" and "know" the Lord.

Learning about God's Attributes

1. Read the quotes by Tozer in the personal study (Study Guide pp. 5-6). Ask the following questions:

   a. What relationship does Tozer draw between our concept of God and our Christian walk?

   b. Is this a valid claim? Why or why not?

2. Read the following definition of the word *attribute*: "a characteristic or quality of a person or thing" (*Webster's New World Dictionary*, Third College Edition, Simon & Schuster, 1988). Discuss with the class how learning about God's attributes can improve our concept of Him.

3. If you have not already passed out copies of this book, do so now. Spend a few minutes looking over the various attributes mentioned in the table of contents. Ask, "What attributes especially intrigue you? Why?"

4. From the personal study, explain a little about the life of A.W. Tozer and how this book came to be. You will want to say everything you can to convince your class members that they should read the book chapter by chapter, in its entirety.

Closing

1. Assign the reading of chapter 1 in the book. To whet the appetites of your group, you may want to read a short, incisive quote from the chapter.

2. Close in prayer.

Chapter 1:
God's Infinitude

Personal Study

Supplementary Materials: Julian of Norwich, *Revelations of Divine Love* (New York: Penguin Classics, 1999).

It seems only natural that in speaking of God's attributes, Tozer would start with infinitude. As Tozer defines it, *infinitude* means that "All that God is, He is without bounds or limits" (p. 4). Probably the biggest danger in studying the attributes of God is the possibility of coming to think, if even subconsciously, that we fully *understand* God. Tozer immediately addresses that misconception by pointing out that God is infinite—we can never come to the end of our knowledge of Him.

And yet, isn't it odd that he begins his message with the following Scripture?

> If ye then be risen with Christ, seek those things which are above, where Christ sitteth on the right hand of God. Set your affection on things above, not on things on the earth. For ye are dead, and your life is hid with Christ in God. (Colossians 3:1-3)

9

Strange, isn't it? This passage appears to discuss the believer's position in Christ, rather than God's infinitude. Why does the chapter begin here? The answer to that question is the thread that runs through both volumes of *The Attributes of God*: In every chapter, Tozer endeavors to show how God's attributes relate directly to our life in Him.

The Journey to Infinity

"The last eight words of this verse," Tozer says, "would make a good sermon for anybody: 'Your life is hid with Christ in God' " (pp. 1-2). This hidden life in God is where God's infinitude meets our spiritual need. To illustrate, Tozer quotes from *Revelations of Divine Love* by medieval author Lady Julian of Norwich: "Suddenly the Trinity filled my heart with joy. And I understood that so it shall be in heaven without end" (pp. 1-2). Tozer comments that this is a distinctly different vision of heaven than the "utilitarian" heaven that many people dream about. Read Tozer's description of these two conceptions of heaven on page 2. Which is closer to your concept of heaven?

The hidden life begins, Tozer says, when we realize that "God is all that we would have and can desire" (p. 3). Once we really believe that all we need and desire is found in God alone, the significance of God's infinitude is overwhelming. As Tozer puts it,

Christianity is a gateway into God. And then when you get into God, "with Christ in God," then you're on a journey into infinity, into infinitude. There is no limit and no place to stop. There isn't

just one work of grace, or a second work or a third work, and then that's it. There are *numberless* experiences and spiritual epochs and crises that can take place in your life while you are journeying out into the heart of God in Christ.
God is infinite! That's the hardest thought I will ask you to grasp. You cannot understand what infinite means, but don't let it bother you—I don't understand it and I'm trying to explain it! (pp. 3-4)

Infinity Cannot Be Measured

Tozer tries to help us conceive of the vastness of God's infinitude by showing how different He is from created things. "There is nothing boundless but God and nothing infinite but God. God is self-existent and absolute; everything else is contingent and relative" (p. 5).

My favorite illustration is the one he borrows from C.S. Lewis:

C.S. Lewis said that if you could think of a sheet of paper infinitely extended in all directions, and if you took a pencil and made a line one inch long on it, that would be time. When you started to push your pencil it was the beginning of time and when you lifted it off the paper it was the end of time. And all around, infinitely extended in all directions, is God. (pp. 5-6)

In all of this, Tozer is inviting us to expand our minds—to exercise our imagination—in conceiving God's greatness. No, of course we cannot take in the vastness of God with our small, finite minds, but it's a start toward having a conception of God that is

11

more worthy of Him. Tozer says these kinds of mental exercises are "a mighty good cure for this little cheap god we have today" (p. 7).

In the same way that you evaluated your concept of heaven earlier in this lesson, think about your own concept of God. While no one can hope to conceive of God in a way that even approaches His infinite majesty, ask yourself these questions: Is my concept of God too small? Is it worthy of the God I serve? How would a larger view of God affect the way I live?

God Takes Pleasure in Himself

Some people seem to fear such a high and lofty conception of God because to their minds it makes Him appear cold, impersonal and distant. Tozer, however, has no such fear and no such misconception. This is why he reminds us that God takes pleasure in Himself and in His creation.

> A mother doesn't have to get up and feed her baby at 2 in the morning. . . . She wants to do it. I used to do it for our little fellows, and I enjoyed doing it. A mother and a father do what they do because they love to do it.
>
> It is the same with this awesome, eternal, invisible, infinite, all-wise, omniscient God, the God of our fathers, the God and Father of our Lord Jesus Christ and the God we call "our Father which art in heaven." He is boundless and infinite; He can't be weighed or measured; you can't apply distance or time or space to Him, for He made it all and contains it all in His own heart. While He rises above it all, at the same time this God is a

friendly, congenial God and He delights in Himself. (p. 9)

Does this describe your relationship with God? Is He your infinite but personal, loving Father? Do you know that He delights in you?

God Takes Pleasure in His Work

If there is still any doubt that the infinite God delights in us, Tozer refers to the parable of the lost sheep in Luke 15, in which the shepherd, when he finds the lost sheep, "he layeth it on his shoulders, rejoicing" (15:5).

Tozer says that God has enthusiasm for all His creation. "This infinite God is enjoying Himself. Somebody is having a good time in heaven and earth and sea and sky" (p. 12). In meditating on the vast infinitude of God, we must never for a minute imagine that God's greatness diminishes for one moment His interest and concern for all the works of His hands. This is the great God we serve—infinite, yet intimate.

Singing for Joy

Tozer points out also that there was singing at creation ("the morning stars sang together" [Job 38:7]), and there will be singing at the end of time ("And they sung a new song" [Revelation 5:9]), as well as at other major events in God's eternal plan. All of God's works are a joyful celebration.

This brings us back to the quote from Lady Julian at the beginning of the chapter: "Suddenly the Trinity filled my heart with joy. And I understood that so it shall be in heaven without end" (pp. 1-2). God calls us to join in the celebration with the Father, Son and Holy Spirit. Lady Julian also said, "Where Jesus appeareth, the Blessed Trinity is understood" (p. 2). As Tozer puts it,

> The infinite Godhead invites us into Himself to share in all the intimacies of the Trinity. And Christ is the way in.
>
> The moon and the earth turn in such a way that we only see one side of the moon and never see the other. The eternal God is so vast, so infinite, that I can't hope to know all about God and all there is about God. But God has a manward side, just as the moon has an earthward side. Just as the moon always keeps that smiling yellow face turned earthward, so God has a side He always keeps turned manward, and that side is Jesus Christ. (pp. 15-16)

What can we learn from this study of God's infinitude? We discover a God who is far beyond our comprehension, but one who is intimately concerned for us. More than that, He invites us into relationship with Him. He is the God with whom we will never become bored, the God whom we can know, but will never reach the end of. This is the God we worship!

LESSON PLAN—Group Study

AIM: To help my students understand God's attribute of infinitude and how it applies to their relationships with Him.

Introduction

1. Open with prayer.

2. Have someone read Colossians 3:1-3. Discuss how this passage relates to God's infinitude.

The Journey to Infinity

1. Ask students to find and reread Tozer's definition of God's infinitude in the text of the chapter. (Hint: It's under this subhead.)

2. Discuss what Tozer means by "the journey into infinity." To get the ball rolling, read this statement: "There isn't just one work of grace, or a second work or a third work, and then that's it. There are *numberless* experiences and spiritual epochs and crises that can take place in your life while you are journeying out into the heart of God in Christ" (pp. 3-4).

Infinity Cannot Be Measured

1. Ask students to spend a moment in silent meditation on the illustration by C.S. Lewis (pp. 5-6 in the text).

2. Tozer says that many Christians have an inadequate view of God: "This little cheap god we've made up is one you can pal around with—'the Man upstairs,' the fellow who helps you win baseball games" (p. 7). Is this a fair statement? Discuss.

God Takes Pleasure in Himself

1. Ask the class this question: "Why does Tozer change gears at this point and begin to talk

about God taking pleasure in Himself and the works of His hands?"

2. Read Philippians 2:5-8. Compare this verse to what Tozer says about Christ's attitude toward the incarnation (pp. 9-10).

God Takes Pleasure in His Work

Discuss the following two statements by Tozer:

1. "There is an enthusiasm in the Godhead, and there is enthusiasm in creation" (p. 10).

2. "We ought to stop thinking like scientists and think like psalmists" (p. 12).

Singing for Joy

1. Have the class list the significant acts of God that Tozer says involved singing. Ask if anyone can think of other major biblical events which included singing and rejoicing.

2. Discuss the significance of singing being present in all these events.

Closing

1. Read the paragraph about "the moon and earth" (pp. 15-16). Ask students what they have learned from this study of God's infinitude.

2. Assign reading of chapter 2 in the book.

3. Close in prayer.

Chapter 2:
God's Immensity

Personal Study

Supplementary Materials: Julian of Norwich, *Revelations of Divine Love* (New York: Penguin Classics, 1999).

This particular chapter is unique in that, along with selected Scripture passages, Tozer opens the message with a prayer. And what a prayer it is: "Father, we're unworthy to think these thoughts, and our friends are unworthy to hear them expressed. But we will try to hear worthily and speak worthily. . . . Show Thyself to us, O God!" (pp. 17-18). It is a prayer that would be fitting to precede any of these chapters on God's attributes.

Tozer also lays some groundwork for later chapters with a discussion of two kinds of faith—nominal and real.

The nominal faith is faith that accepts what it is told and can quote text after text to prove it. . . . But there is another kind of faith: it is faith that depends upon the character of God. . . . The man who has real faith rather than nominal faith has found a right answer to the question, "What is God like?" There is no question more important. The man of true faith has found an answer to that question by revelation and illumination.

The difficulty with the Church now—even the Bible-believing Church—is that we stop with revelation. But revelation is not enough. (pp. 18-19)

Illumination

The point that Tozer is getting at is that revelation (the written Word of God) must be supplemented by illumination of the Word by the Holy Spirit. "The given revelation is a means toward an end, and God is the end, not the text itself" (p. 19). He makes a similar point in a chapter from *The Root of the Righteous* entitled "Bible Taught or Spirit Taught?":

> It is altogether possible to be instructed in the rudiments of the faith and still have no real understanding of the whole thing. And it is possible to go on to become expert in Bible doctrine and not have spiritual illumination, with the result that a veil remains over the mind, preventing it from apprehending the truth in its spiritual essence.

What does all this have to do with God's immensity? Tozer is emphasizing again that the purpose of learning the attributes of God is not merely to know *about* God, but to know God Himself. (Remember the opening prayer? "Show Thyself to us, O God!") And this is of particular importance when looking at God's immensity, as we will see.

The Size of Things

Tozer again refers to the book *Revelations of Divine Love* by Lady Julian of Norwich, in which she describes a vision she had of "a very small object as large as a hazelnut" (p. 20). When she asked what it might be, it was revealed to her that "this is all that is made"—all creation, the entire universe. God was showing her what the universe looks like from His perspective.

Compare this to what Tozer quotes Pascal as saying about the human perspective on the size of things: "We are halfway between immensity and that which is infinitesimally small" (p. 20). Comparatively speaking, human beings are creation's midpoint between the vastness of space and the minuteness of the atom. "There is no way to prove that," Tozer admits, "but that's a frightening place to be, half as big as the universe but also half as small" (p. 21).

It is tempting to begin to draw some conclusions at this point, but Tozer has still another perspective on God's relation to the universe for us to think about.

The Immanence of God

The attribute of *immanence* (which is addressed in more detail in chapter 8), is that God is everywhere and in everything, penetrating and permeating all the universe. This is a different attribute than God's omnipresence (which, by the way, is covered in chapter 7). "*There isn't any place where God is not*" (p. 22), as Tozer puts it.

The Immensity of God

And yet, Tozer adds, God is so immense that the universe cannot contain Him. Though He is in everything, He is not confined or contained by His creation. Instead, He contains it. As an exercise to see how this view of God stands up against Scripture, meditate on Isaiah 40. Note how certain verses relate to what Tozer has said so far about God's immensity. It is especially interesting to compare verse 15 to Lady Julian's vision of the hazelnut.

God Holds What He Loves

When the universe is seen in this perspective, you may wonder, along with Lady Julian and Tozer, what holds it all together. The answer, of course, is God. "God loves that which He made. And because He made it, He loves it, and because He loves it, He keeps it" (p. 27). The picture Tozer paints for us is a Creator God who lovingly nurtures and cherishes all that He has made, "upholding all things by the word of his power" (Hebrews 1:3).

Why Are We Not Happy?

Knowing that God keeps us by His power should make us the happiest people in the world, Lady Julian says. So why aren't we? The answer to this question, and the whole point of this chapter, is: *We depend on the world—that little hazelnut—to make us happy, rather than God.* We try to find pleasure in things that are too small, which only leaves us unsatisfied.

Then, after cluttering our lives with things, we want to add God to the mix. As Tozer puts it, we try to have God with a plus sign—God plus this, or God plus that—which can never work:

> You're made in the image of God, and nothing short of God will satisfy you. And even if you happen to be one of those "nickel-in-the-slot, get saved, escape hell and take heaven" Christians (that poor little kinder-garten view of heaven), remember one thing—even you will find over the years that you are not content with "things plus God." You'll have to have God mi-nus all things. (p. 30)

It may sound like Tozer is calling us to live like a hermit in a cave—and certainly, a misunderstand-ing of this truth is probably the source of much of the extremism in some eras of church history. But Tozer is saying that we can have things, and even love things as gifts from God, as long as we do not make them necessary to our happiness.

In what ways do you depend on the things of the world for your happiness? Could your faith survive the loss of all things?

God's Enthusiasm

Returning to a theme from chapter 1, Tozer re-minds us that God is enthusiastic about His cre-ation—especially *us*, the one part of His creation that is made in His own image. But because, as Tozer says, "we don't believe that God is delighted, infinitely delighted with us" (p. 32), we find it hard to have the same enthusiasm for Him.

Such enthusiasm is the key to revival, when we can honestly pray with Lady Julian, "Oh God, give me Thyself! For nothing less than Thee will do" (p. 32). Such a prayer is worth praying every day.

Hunger for God

In her medieval way of wording it, Lady Julian says that anything less than God Himself "ever me wanteth," which means "it won't be enough" (p. 32). This hunger for God—in most people, unknown and unexpressed—is what Tozer sees as the root cause of mental illness, murder, suicide and other human miseries.

> This is the greatest calamity for a human soul: to be made in the image of God, with a spirit so big that it can contain the universe, and yet cry for more. Imagine a soul bigger than the heavens and the heaven of heavens yet empty of God. Imagine going through eternity crying, "Ever me wanteth, O God"—forever and ever! . . .
>
> I wonder if the flames of hell aren't kindled from deep in that shrine [of the heart] where, dry and cracked and parched, the soul of man cries, "O God, *ever me wanteth*. I've had everything: religion, position, money, a spouse and children, clothes, a good home; but it's a little hazelnut—it's nothing. O God, I've missed that which I wanted the most!" (pp. 33-34)

God Must Be First

Jesus said it was worthless to gain the whole world if you lose your soul (Mark 8:36). Tozer points out that this doesn't mean you can just "add on" God to a life full of other loves—He must be first, and all in all. This is the only way your life can truly be "hid with Christ in God" (Colossians 3:3). Then God may bless you with things, such as money, education, family and friends—but only with the understanding that He can take them away, that they will never try to usurp the throne of your heart.

Just as he began this message, Tozer closes with a prayer. It is one well worth praying ourselves:

> *Now, Father, wilt Thou bless all who receive this message? Wilt Thou grant, we pray, that we may forget the things that are behind and press forward toward the things that are ahead? Wilt Thou grant that we may see all that is as only the size of a hazelnut and ourselves in God as vast, so vast that we encompass the worlds and are utterly empty without Thee? Fill us, O God, fill us with Thyself, for without Thee ever we will be wanting. Fill us with Thyself for Jesus Christ's sake. Amen.* (p. 37)

LESSON PLAN—Group Study

AIM: To help my students understand how God's immensity is reflected in the emptiness of our hearts that only He can fill.

Introduction

1. Open with prayer.

2. Have someone read the three passages at the beginning of the chapter (Matthew 16:25-26; Colossians 3:3; Philippians 3:8). Discuss what the common theme of these passages is. Ask if the opening prayer (pp. 17-18) gives a hint of that common theme.

3. Ask the class to identify what Tozer means by *nominal faith* and *real faith*.

Illumination

Tozer says a proper answer to the question, "What is God like?" is found through illumination of the Word of God by the Holy Spirit. Ask the class how this relates to God's immensity (see the personal study [*Study Guide*, p. 18]).

The Size of Things

Discuss Lady Julian's vision of all created things being "the size of a hazelnut." Ask how this vision changes one's perspective.

The Immanence of God

Have someone read Psalm 139:8-10, then have someone read the definition of *immanence* as given in the personal study (*Study Guide*, p. 19). Discuss.

The Immensity of God

Have someone read Isaiah 40, with special emphasis on verse 15. Based on this Scripture, ask how God's immensity differs from God's immanence.

God Holds What He Loves

Discuss Tozer's explanation for why things do not fall apart: God made them, God loves them, God keeps them. What significance does this have for our lives?

Why Are We Not Happy?

Ask the group these questions: Why does seeking after things leave us unsatisfied? What is the solution?

God's Enthusiasm

Discuss why Tozer brings up "God's enthusiasm"—a theme from the previous chapter. How does it apply to our need to seek after Him?

Hunger for God

Ask if anyone in the group has experienced the heart-hunger for God that Tozer describes. Invite them to share their testimonies.

God Must Be First

Discuss the difference between trying to "add on God" and having your life "hid with Christ in God."

Closing

1. Read the prayer at the end of chapter 2 together.

2. Assign chapter 3 to read for next week's class.

3. Close in prayer.

Chapter 3:
God's Goodness

Personal Study

Supplementary Materials: Julian of Norwich, *Revelations of Divine Love* (New York: Penguin Classics, 1999); David J. Fant, Jr., *A.W. Tozer: A Twentieth-Century Prophet* (Camp Hill, PA: WingSpread Publishers, 1964; reprint, 2002).

Early in this chapter on God's goodness, Tozer poses a very provocative statement: "Christianity at any given time is strong or weak depending on her concept of God" (p. 41). Tozer goes on to suggest that the Christianity of his era was weak because of an unworthy view of God. That was nearly fifty years ago, but is there any evidence that our popular concept of God has improved?

Tozer also refers disparagingly to "cowboy religion," by which he most likely meant the tendency of Christians to imitate the latest Hollywood fads, which at that time included westerns and country ballads (see, for example, the essay quoted in David Fant's biography of Tozer, pages 143-144). What do you think is the modern equivalent of "cowboy religion"?

The solution to a shallow concept of God, Tozer says, is to "magnify the LORD" (Psalm 34:3). The word *magnify*, in this sense, means to see God bigger, to change our concept of Him to something closer to reality—although we need to recognize that the infinite God can never be fully comprehended by our finite and fallen minds.

All this is presented to set the stage for a more realistic view of God's goodness.

What "Good" Means

Tozer probably began by expressing concern for our concept of God because *goodness* is the first of the attributes he discusses that we can possess as well—which immediately puts us in danger of seeing God in human terms. It's easier to properly understand an attribute of God such as infinitude, which is possessed solely by Him alone. But those attributes such as God's goodness, which can be part of the redeemed human personality (sometimes called the "moral attributes" by theologians), can be misunderstood. We can easily slip into thinking of human goodness, which cannot begin to describe God's goodness.

That is why Tozer explains how the different attributes of God interact with each other. For example, God is infinite. Therefore, if He is good, He is *infinitely* good. If He is immutable (He never changes), then He is *immutably* good. So while we possess (in a redeemed person, at least) the ability to be good, we must not confuse that with the infinite, unchanging goodness of God.

A true understanding of God's goodness disproves deism, which Tozer defines as the concept of God as "an absentee engineer running His world by remote control" (p. 44). But the goodness of God is such that He cannot be indifferent about His creation. Isn't it great to know that God is actively involved in the universe as an expression of His goodness?

Our Reason for Living

The answer to every question, Tozer contends, is "God out of His goodness willed it" (p. 46). It is the reason why we were created, why God did not destroy Adam and Eve when they fell and why God sent His only Son to die on the cross for our sins. The operative word here is *grace*—God's undeserved favor, showered on us for no other reason than that He is good.

It is also why God answers our prayers. It is probably a great blow to the theology of some people to hear Tozer declare, "Nobody ever got anything from God on the grounds that he deserved it" (p. 47). The interesting thing, however, is that it puts us all on the same plane. There are no great saints whose prayers God answers because of their merit. They are no more deserving than any of the rest of us. We are all eligible for God's grace. Why? Because He is good!

Tozer sounds a similar note in his book *Christ the Eternal Son*:

Let us remember this: Everything God does is by grace, for no man, no creature, no being deserves anything. Salvation is by grace, the Creation is by grace—all that God does is by grace and every human being has received of His fullness.

This boundless grace must operate wherever that which is not God appeals to that which is God; wherever the voice of the creature crosses the vast gulf to the ears of the Creator. . . .

All that you have is out of His grace. Jesus Christ, the eternal Word, who became flesh and dwelt among us, is the open channel through which God moves to provide all the benefits He gives to saints and sinners.

And what about the years, the rest of your existence?

You cannot believe that you have earned it.

You cannot believe that it has something to do with whether you are good or bad.

Confess that it is out of His grace, for the entire universe is the beneficiary of God's grace and goodness.

Goodness and Severity

What about those who reject His goodness? We can do this because we have free will—or, as Tozer calls it, "provisional sovereignty" (p. 48). We have a small measure of authority (small in comparison to God's absolute authority) over our lives, to choose whether to serve God or ourselves, whether to go to heaven or hell.

Even here, however, God in His goodness has provided for us. Tozer quotes again from Lady Julian: "God of His goodness has ordained means to help us, full, fair and many; the chief being that which He took upon Him, the nature of man" (p. 49). The ability of God to sympathize and empathize with us is found in Hebrews 2:17-18 and 4:15-16. His provision for our redemption has the effect of (in Julian's words) "turning all our blame into endless worship" (p. 51).

We Can Boldly Approach Him

God's goodness means we can be bold—almost arrogant, Tozer says—in our prayers to God. And Tozer emphasizes again that it has nothing to do with his own merit before God. "I'm not a good man. . . . I can't go to God and say, 'God, I didn't do what that fellow did.' I've done everything—either in actuality or in thought—that could be done" (p. 51). And he loves God all the more, because "he who is forgiven much loves much" (see Luke 7:47).

God's Kindness

Tozer reminds us that "Jesus is God. And Jesus is the kindest man ever to live on this earth" (p. 52). This is why we cannot view human kindness and hope to get an idea of what God's kindness is like. All human examples pale in comparison. Like the father who accepted his wayward child home in the parable of the prodigal son, God is not revolted by our wretchedness. He sees us as perfect even though we are not—out of His goodness.

God Wants to Please Us

Jesus came to end all human tears. He wants us to take pleasure in Him. Tozer's advice—which he repeats a second time for emphasis—is, "Let's put away all doubts and trust Him" (p. 56).

It's funny how our doubts about God's goodness seem to center on ourselves—"How could God be good to me, as bad as I am?" Some would say we are suffering from low self-esteem and we need to pump ourselves up until we think we *deserve* His goodness! But instead of magnifying ourselves—trying to believe the lie that we are bigger than we really are—we should magnify God. We should strive to see Him as big as He is, as good as He is—so good that He loves us even in our wretchedness. Think of all the effort God has gone through—and continues to go through—to take us out of our wretchedness and prepare us to be with Him in heaven. This is why Tozer's wrap-up to this chapter, though a very startling thought, rings true: "Did you ever stop to think that God is going to be as pleased to have you with Him in heaven as you are to be there?" (p. 56). Praise God for His goodness!

LESSON PLAN—Group Study

AIM: To help my students understand the immensity of God's goodness to us, especially in His gift of salvation.

Introduction

1. Open with prayer.

2. Have the group discuss this statement by Tozer: "Christianity at any given time is strong or weak depending upon her concept of God" (p. 41).

3. Ask the group what Tozer meant by "cowboy religion." Is there a modern equivalent to that?

What "Good" Means

Have someone read the seven Scripture passages at the beginning of the chapter (Psalm 119:68; Isaiah 63:7; Psalm 139:17; Deuteronomy 30:9; Psalm 36:7; Psalm 34:8; Matthew 7:11). Ask, "How does God's goodness differ from our own?"

Our Reason for Living

Have the class list some of the things we—as believers, but also as beings created by God—have because of God's goodness and grace. Save this list for the closing, when you will spend time as a group thanking God for His goodness.

Goodness and Severity

Have someone read Hebrews 2:17-18 and 4:15-16. Discuss what blessings have come to us as a result of the Son of God taking on human nature.

We Can Boldly Approach Him

Discuss what Tozer means by being bold in our prayers to God. How does it relate to his later confession of his sinfulness?

God's Kindness

Read from the book the first paragraph under this heading (pp. 52-55). Ask, "How should the knowledge of the greatness of God's kindness affect the way we live?"

God Wants to Please Us

Discuss Tozer's repeated statement, "Let's put away all doubts and trust Him" (p. 56). What is Tozer asking us to trust God about?

Closing

1. Read the last two paragraphs of the chapter (pp. 56-57). Spend some time as a group praising God for His goodness.

2. Assign chapter 4 to read for next week's class.

3. Close in prayer.

Chapter 4:
God's Justice

Personal Study

Supplementary Materials: Anselm, *Anselm of Canterbury: The Major Works* (Oxford: Oxford Univ. Press, 1998).

In seeking to define justice, Tozer makes the declaration that "Justice is indistinguishable from righteousness in the Old Testament" (p. 60). I checked a concordance and found that he is absolutely correct; the *same* Hebrew word is translated "justice" in some verses and "righteousness" in others.

Tozer is also right that the Hebrew word for righteousness/justice has an implied meaning of "equal" or "equity." And he points out that, by contrast, the word *iniquity* means "unequal." That is why Ezekiel 18:25 says, "Hear now, O house of Israel; Is not my way equal? are not your ways unequal?" There is so much here that Tozer only touches on; the idea of God being "morally equal" could be a sermon in itself.

When Tozer tells us that God is not only just, He is justice, it is more than mere semantics (or poor grammar!). God is actually just in a different way than we are. We are just if we more or less follow a standard of justice outside ourselves—a biblical and godly standard, we hope. But God doesn't follow a standard; He *is* the standard. When Tozer says that God is justice, he means God invented the idea. So when someone says that justice *requires* God to do something, it's a nonsense statement, similar to saying that my son *requires* me to be a father!

Tozer defines judgment as "the application of justice to a moral situation" (p. 61). God, being morally equal, is not ever off-balance or unfair in His judgments. All things will be made equal in the end, and everyone will get what they deserve. But isn't that the very thing we ought to be afraid of? If heaven were only for those who deserved it, how many of us would qualify?

This is why Tozer presents us with the question that Anselm posed in his *Proslogium*: "How dost Thou spare the wicked if Thou art just?" (p. 63). Tozer says that we do not worry about this question anymore, because we have "cheapened salvation" by making it into a cold, legal transaction. It seems to me that another reason we do not ask Anselm's question today is because we do not think of ourselves—or hardly any other person, for that matter—as truly "wicked," so the question of how God spares the wicked is a moot point. (Such an attitude is in itself rather wicked, don't you think?)

At any rate, Tozer rightly declares that this question is worth considering, and he presents three answers to it.

1. The Unity of God

One answer to Anselm's question is wrapped up in the nature of God—specifically, His oneness.

God is not made of parts, the way we are. "Hear, O Israel: The LORD our God is one" (Deuteronomy 6:4). Because of this, His various attributes do not "quarrel with each other" (p. 65), as Tozer puts it. God doesn't ever have a split personality.

God is just, but spares the wicked because of the oneness of His nature. In other words, His justice and His mercy are not at war with each other; they are both expressions of His one nature. God is all mercy, but *at the same time* is all justice. While humans have to harmonize these attitudes within themselves, God does not have to harmonize them, because they are never in conflict with each other in the first place.

So the answer as to how God can be just and spare the wicked is wrapped up in the unity of God; His justice and mercy are one.

2. The Passion of Christ

A second answer Tozer gives to Anselm's question is one we all know and understand—or at least we think we do. Christ's passion (deep, terrible suffering) on the cross canceled the debt of sin. Tozer ties the unity of God to the passion of Christ on the cross and points out that the atonement for sin through the blood of Christ is "infinite, almighty and perfect" (p. 67). "You never can exaggerate the power of the cross" (p. 68), he declares.

Tozer also calls on the unity of God to dispel a misunderstanding about Christ's death: "Jesus Christ did not die to change God; Jesus Christ died to change a moral situation" (p. 70). The cross did *not* change God's mind about us; it changed our moral situation. We were lost in our sin; God in His justice sentenced us to die—a decision that does not quarrel with His mercy, kindness or compassion. But when the sinner turns from his sin and turns to God, accepting Christ's death on the cross as payment for his sin, God in His mercy gives that sinner eternal life—a decision that does not quarrel with His justice.

Tozer is very concerned that we get rid of any idea of God's mercy and justice "fighting" with each other, because that would imply that God was in conflict with Himself—an impossibility, since God is unified. "The idea that the cross wiped the angry scowl off the face of God and He began grudgingly to smile is a pagan concept and not Christian" (p. 72).

That is why Tozer can say with assurance that: "Justice is on the side of the returning sinner" (p. 71). Those who repent and turn to God can be confident of His mercy and grace, for justification by faith is *always* how God has dealt with man.

Even in the Old Testament, David proclaimed forgiveness to those who repent and confess:

> Blessed is he whose transgression is forgiven, whose sin is covered. Blessed is the man unto whom the LORD imputeth not iniquity, and in whose spirit there is no guile. When I kept silence, my bones waxed old through my roaring all the day long. For day and night thy hand was heavy upon me: my moisture is turned into the drought of summer. Selah. I acknowledged my sin unto thee, and mine iniquity have I not hid. I said, I will confess my transgressions unto the LORD; and thou forgavest the iniquity of my sin. (Psalm 32:1-5)

3. *The Unchanging God*

Anselm's question can also be answered by appealing to the unchanging nature of God. He is and always has been just and loving and good. Tozer points out how God's attributes, far from "fighting" with each other, perfectly complement each other. His attribute of goodness implies His attribute of justice, because if He were not just, He could not possibly be good.

Tozer points out an interesting irony about God's justice: While punishing the wicked is just, because they get what they deserve, pardoning and justifying the wicked is also just, "because it is consistent with God's nature" (pp. 72-73)—God's attributes of compassion and mercy. The wicked, unrepentant sinner is justly condemned to hell, but the repentant, believing sinner is justly given the gift of eternal life. And all of this is because "always God acts like God" (p. 73). He is always consistent.

As a result, Tozer assures us, we who have believed in His Son will be ushered into heaven, to enjoy "the kingdom prepared for [us] from the foundation of the world" (Matthew 25:34). We won't have to sneak in the back door or get in there by accident. We should rejoice over this every day, and join with Tozer in exclaiming with awe, "Oh, the wonder and the mystery and the glory of the being of God!" (p. 74).

LESSON PLAN—Group Study

AIM: To help my students understand God's justice, and especially to see that it does not conflict with His mercy and forgiveness to repentant sinners.

Introduction

1. Open with prayer.

2. Have someone read the seven Scripture passages at the beginning of the chapter (Genesis 18:25; Deuteronomy 10:17; Psalm 19:9; Psalm 92:15; 97:2; Isaiah 28:17; Revelation 16:5-7).

3. Ask the group these two questions:
   • What is the common definition of justice, according to most people?
   • What is Tozer's definition of God's justice, and is it different than the common definition?

4. Read the following question posed by Anselm: "How can God be just and still spare the wicked?"

Before covering Tozer's three-pronged response to that question, have the class discuss whether believers ask this kind of question very often, and why or why not.

1. The Unity of God

Discuss the concept that "Man is made of parts," but "God is unitary" (pp. 64-65). How does this make us different from God? How does it affect our ability to understand God's justice? Ask Anselm's question again. How does the concept of God's unity answer this question?

2. The Passion of Christ

Ask "What does Tozer mean when he says, 'Jesus Christ died to change a moral situation'?" (p. 70). Ask Anselm's question again. How does the concept of Christ's passion answer this question?

3. The Unchanging God

Discuss what it means to say that God acts in a way consistent with His nature. Ask Anselm's question again. How does the concept of God's unchanging nature answer this question?

Closing

1. Read the last two paragraphs of the chapter (p. 74). Take a moment as a class to thank God that *in His justice* He saved us from our sins.

2. Assign chapter 5 to read for next week's class.

3. Close in prayer.

Chapter 5:
God's Mercy

Personal Study

Supplementary Materials: A.W. Tozer, *Faith Beyond Reason* (Camp Hill, PA: WingSpread Publishers, 1989); C.S. Lewis, *Mere Christianity* (New York: Simon and Schuster, 1996).

Chapters 5 and 6 deal with mercy and grace—two of God's attributes that are so closely linked that it takes a theologian to distinguish between them. That's what this study of God's attributes is making of us, if we define a *theologian* as someone who is trying to get to know and understand God better. (Too many people consider *theologian* as just another word for *Pharisee*, but nothing could be further from the truth. If the Pharisees had been better theologians, they would have followed Christ!)

It makes sense, therefore, that early in the chapter Tozer should define mercy: "to stoop in kindness to an inferior, to have pity upon and to be actively compassionate" (p. 79). But first, he endeavors to set down a biblical base to build on. The four passages he quotes at the beginning (Psalm 103:8-17; 2 Corinthians 1:3; James 5:11; and 2 Peter 3:9) are carefully chosen. Take a moment to reread them now. Notice that they are by four different authors—David, Paul, James and Peter—but they all have the same theme: that God is merciful *to us*, not dealing with us according to our sins. It is interesting that Peter's passage doesn't even use the word *mercy*— but it doesn't have to, does it? It is dripping with God's mercy!

The next two passages he quotes (Exodus 34:4-7; 2 Chronicles 5:13-14) are to show that God's mercy is eternal and infinite (which is not surprising; if there is one thing we have learned from the past few lessons, it is that all of God's attributes reflect His unified nature). Both of these passages are from the Old Testament, because Tozer also wants to make the point that God has *always* been compassionate and merciful—not just since Jesus came.

The idea "that the Old Testament is a book of severity and law, and the New Testament is a book of tenderness and grace" (p. 77) is a heresy that goes back to the early Church. Marcion, whose erroneous teachings became a major threat to Christianity in the second century, took this notion to its logical conclusion and said that the God of the Old Testament was a *different* God than the God of the New Testament!

Tozer is very concerned that we do not fall into this error of pitting one part of the Bible against another, and so he points out that the word *mercy* is used four times more often in the Old Testament than in the New. This is true; in fact, Tozer understates the case. When the words *mercies* and *merciful* are taken into account, the ratio is even higher on the side of the Old Testament.

God's mercy is an outgrowth of His goodness, His "urge . . . to bestow blessedness" (p. 78). Calling on Isaiah 63:7-9 and Ezekiel 33:11, Tozer shows that God takes pleasure in blessing, not in cursing. Though in His justice He may deem it necessary to punish, He doesn't enjoy it. That reminds me of a story C.S. Lewis told in *Mere Christianity* about a schoolboy who was asked what God was like. He said that God was the kind of person who was always trying to stop people from enjoying themselves! We may laugh at that, but don't we sometimes fall into that kind of thinking? We need to see God as "a God full of compassion, and gracious, long-suffering, and plenteous in mercy and truth" (Psalm 86:15).

The mercy of God, Tozer says, is "to be actively compassionate" (p. 80), a concept that seems to be lost in the world today. In Exodus 2:23-25, God's compassion moved Him to help the Israelites. In Mark 6:34, Jesus' compassion for the multitudes moved Him to feed them (6:37 ff.). While some people are compassionate "for a minute and a half" (p. 81), as Tozer puts it, they do not let it move them to action. But God's compassion and mercy led Him to action—ultimately, to die on a cross for the whole world.

God's mercy always was and always will be. It did not begin because Jesus died; Jesus died because of

God's desire to show mercy. Because it is boundless and immeasurable, there is nothing that we or anyone else can do to increase or decrease God's mercy. "No attribute of God is greater than any other" (p. 83). But Tozer makes an important point: God's mercy may seem "bigger" than other attributes because *we need it so much.* "Our need determines which of God's attributes at the moment we'll celebrate" (p. 85).

The Operation of God's Mercy

Tozer then suggests another definition of God's mercy, with the emphasis on how it operates in our lives: "Mercy is God's goodness confronting human guilt and suffering" (p. 85). When God's justice confronts our sin, it results in judgment. In the same way, when God's goodness confronts our guilt and suffering, it results in mercy. We all receive God's mercy, no matter who we are, because otherwise we would have perished a long time ago (Lamentations 3:22). God could destroy the whole world, but because of His mercy, He is holding off judgment to give the unbeliever a chance to repent and come to faith in Christ (Romans 2:4, 2 Peter 3:9).

Mercy holds off judgment, but it does not cancel it. That can only happen through atonement, Tozer reminds us. Mercy brought Christ to the cross, but the actual how and why of Christ's death on the cross remains a mystery; Tozer says he doesn't understand it.

In a theology class, you would be likely to hear of various "theories of the atonement" to explain the mystery. I don't think Tozer would be opposed to such theories, as long as we recognize that even the most comprehensive theological explanation is a crude attempt to discuss something beyond our comprehension. I like how Tozer explains what happened on the cross:

> Justification means that mercy and justice have collaborated so that when God turns and sees iniquity, and then sees the man of iniquity rushing to the cross, He no longer sees iniquity but justification. And so we're justified by faith. (p. 87)

The Suffering of God

Another thing beyond our comprehension is the aspect of mercy in which God participates in our sufferings: "In all their affliction he was afflicted" (Isaiah 63:9). But if affliction and suffering mean one is lacking something or is disordered, how can *God* suffer? Tozer says it is something we have to take on faith. We have to learn to accept that our little minds cannot always comprehend, and join with Ezekiel in saying, "O, Lord GOD, thou knowest" (Ezekiel 37:3).

One problem of believers today, Tozer says, is that we think we know it all. "We're too slick; we have too many answers" (p. 88). True spiritual wisdom, however, is learning to accept what we cannot completely understand. Just because we can't understand how it works, we can still appreciate it, just as we can use our eyes and ears even though we don't really understand how they work.

Tozer adds that some hymn writers have foolishly talked of hoping to someday know why God loves them, but they can't know. All they can know is that "God is love" (1 John 4:16). Why does God have mercy on you? Because God *is* mercy. Don't ask why! We have to just take on faith the fact of the divine empathy and believe that He "makes their bed in their sickness" (see Psalm 41:3). When we suffer, God suffers along with us.

The Nearness of God's Mercy

After quoting Psalm 103:13, that says God's mercy is showered on us "as a father pitieth his children," Tozer tells the story of a World War I refugee who committed suicide so that his child would be cared for as an orphan. "That," he says, "is mercy."

The obvious comparison is Jesus going to His death on a cross for us. In *Faith Beyond Reason*, Tozer speaks of it this way:

> What made Jesus' death uncommon, unusual? It was the dying of the just for the unjust. It was His sacrificial dying, His vicarious dying. He paid a debt He did not owe in behalf of others too deeply in debt ever to pay.

Jesus didn't *have* to die on the cross—He *chose* to! As a father pities his children, Jesus loved and pitied us enough to die in our place.

Our Response to God's Mercy

Tozer encourages us to show mercy because we have received mercy. Think for a moment about ways we can show mercy to others. If nothing comes to mind, think of how God shows us mercy every day.

That is one way we can respond to God's mercy. Another way is to tell God our troubles. Tozer reminds us that the Lord understands with a few lines from an unidentified hymn "written around the book of Hebrews" (p. 92):

> Our Fellow Sufferer still retains
> A fellow feeling of our pains,
>
> . . . .
>
> With boldness, therefore, at the throne
> Let us make all our sorrows known. (pp. 92-93)

What an invitation Tozer gives us as a conclusion to this chapter! "Let us plunge out into the mercy of God and come to know it" (p. 95). Why? Because we need it!

LESSON PLAN—Group Study

AIM: To help my students understand God's mercy, and to learn to trust in His mercy in time of need.

Introduction

1. Open with prayer.

2. Have someone read the Scripture passages at the beginning of the chapter (Psalm 103:8-17; 2 Corinthians 1:3; James 5:11; and 2 Peter 3:9). Ask the group what theme is being expressed about God's mercy (it is to *us*).

3. Read the next two passages (Exodus 34:4-7; 2 Chronicles 5:13-14). Ask what main point is being made about God's mercy (it is eternal and infinite).

4. Read Tozer's definition of mercy at the bottom of page 79. Discuss whether this is an adequate definition. What does it mean to be "actively compassionate"? How can we live this out in our own lives? Ask for real-life examples.

5. Ask if anyone has ever caught themselves taking a dim view of the Old Testament because of its "severity," or unconsciously adopting the schoolboy's idea of God as a "party pooper." (If you as the teacher can confess to either of these attitudes, it may help others to admit it as well.) Ask if this chapter on the mercy of God has helped them to combat these false ideas.

The Operation of God's Mercy

Read aloud Tozer's operative definition of mercy from page 85: "Mercy is God's goodness confronting human guilt and suffering." Have the class discuss how they might put that in their own words. How does Tozer's later statement on that same page—"All men are recipients of God's mercy"—apply to this definition?

The Suffering of God

Tozer says he cannot understand how God could suffer and still be the infinite, perfect being that He is. Ask the group if they have a problem understanding this as well, and if Tozer's decision to believe without understanding is a satisfactory conclusion.

The Nearness of God's Mercy

Have someone read Psalm 103:13. Discuss the story of the World War I refugee and his child. How does this story help us understand the nature of God?

Our Response to God's Mercy

Discuss with the class practical ways that we can show mercy to others, as well as ways we can "plunge into" God's mercy.

Closing

1. Take some time in silent prayer as a group, telling God your troubles and asking Him to show you how to appropriate His mercy.

2. Assign chapter 6 to read for next week's class.

3. Close in prayer.

Chapter 6:
God's Grace

Personal Study

Supplementary Materials: A.W. Tozer, *The Root of the Righteous* (Camp Hill, PA: WingSpread Publishers, 1955, 1986); A.W. Tozer, *Whatever Happened to Worship?* (Camp Hill, PA: WingSpread Publishers, 1985).

Don't be surprised if you have a sense of déjà vu while studying this chapter. Grace is a very similar attribute to mercy, but it's not the same. Review the eight Scripture passages at the beginning of the chapter. Then look at the passages at the beginning of the previous chapter. Do you begin to see the difference between mercy and grace? If not, read on. It should start to become more clear as you continue the study.

Grace Flows from God's Goodness

Like mercy, grace flows from God's goodness. Tozer makes the distinction this way: "Mercy . . . is God's goodness confronting human guilt, whereas grace is God's goodness confronting human demerit"

(p. 98). That is a definition from God's perspective. A preacher once told me a good way of distinguishing the two from the human point of view: mercy is when God doesn't give us what we deserve (punishment); grace is when God gives us what we don't deserve (blessing). God's justice declares the sinner guilty, but mercy holds back the judgment we deserve. God's justice declares us unworthy of the least of His favors, but grace "is that in God which brings into favor one justly in disfavor" (p. 99).

To "bring into favor one justly in disfavor" is a good way to put it, because, as Tozer points out, the KJV uses "grace" and "favor" interchangeably. For example, in Luke 1:30, the angel announces to Mary that she has found "favor" with God, while in Ephesians 2:8 we are told that we are saved by "grace"— but it's the same Greek word!

Tozer notes that the New Testament uses the word *grace* three times more often than the Old Testament, but just as he said in the last chapter about mercy, he emphasizes that grace is the way God has always operated. This certainly makes sense, if grace is an attribute of God; since God doesn't change, He must have always operated in grace, and always will.

Some people think that John 1:17 ("The law was given by Moses, but grace and truth came by Jesus Christ") means Moses knew nothing about grace. That can easily be proven wrong by such verses as Exodus 33:13 and 17, but it can also be proven wrong just by a careful reading of John 1:17 itself. Notice that it says that "grace *and truth* came by Jesus Christ." If we say this verse means that Moses knew nothing about grace, does it mean that he knew nothing about truth, either? We have to understand this verse as saying that Jesus Christ is the channel of grace and truth, and has been *since before the foundation of the world.*

Grace: The Only Means of Salvation

Tozer continues this theme in his discussion of salvation. His two main points are: No one ever was, is or will be saved, except by grace; and "grace always comes by Jesus Christ" (p. 101). "Grace came from the ancient beginnings through Jesus Christ the eternal Son and was manifest on the cross of Calvary" (p. 102). This is why Jesus is referred to as "the Lamb slain *from the foundation of the world*" (Revelation 13:8). The way of salvation was planned ahead of time.

Saving grace operates through faith in Christ; it is the privilege only of those who have experienced the new birth. But Tozer reminds us that a measure of grace is given to everyone. If it were not for grace, judgment would fall; but He gives them a chance to repent. "If thou, LORD, shouldest mark iniquities, O Lord, who shall stand?" (Psalm 130:3). I admire Tozer's willingness to lump himself in with Judas and Hitler as he concludes rather ruefully, "I wonder if there's much difference in us sinners after all" (p. 102).

Grace Is What God Is Like

God is always good and gracious to all peoples everywhere, at all times; there is no meanness, resentment or hardness in God, Tozer assures us. Grace is not just something He wears like a cloak; it's what He is in His nature, to the core of His being. This section of the chapter reminds me of an essay by Tozer in *The Root of the Righteous* entitled "God Is Easy to Live With." It's a message every Christian ought to be reminded of occasionally. Here is just a portion of it:

> It is most important to our spiritual welfare that we hold in our minds always a right conception of God. If we think of Him as cold and exacting we shall find it impossible to love Him, and our lives will be ridden with servile fear. If, again, we hold Him to be kind and understanding our whole inner life will mirror that idea.
>
> The truth is that God is the most winsome of all beings and His service one of unspeakable pleasure. He is all love, and those who trust Him need never know anything but that love. He is just, indeed, and He will not condone sin; but through the blood of the everlasting covenant He is able to act toward us exactly as if we had never sinned. Toward the trusting sons of men His mercy will always triumph over justice.

Is Tozer getting soft on sin? No softer than God! It is true that judgment will still fall on those who refuse to repent, yet there will still be grace.

Grace is immeasurable, like all of God's attributes. And Tozer tells us that if we want to see how great God's grace is, we should measure it against our sin: "But where sin abounded, grace did much more abound" (Romans 5:20). He adds that the phrase, "much more abound" is a colossal understatement—an accommodation to our finite minds. Remember in chapter 1 it was said that "God has no degrees"? We are comparing the finite (our sin) with the infinite (God's grace). God's grace is so vast "that nobody can ever grasp it or hope to understand it" (p. 105).

No matter how much we have sinned, grace abounds to us. Tozer says we should be continually overwhelmed by the immensity of God's grace to us—we who stood under the judgment of sin—so that we would have the right perspective on life. "If we could only remember it [the immensity of God's grace], we wouldn't have to be played with and entertained so much" (p. 105).

How to Look at Grace

Tozer has clearly shown how we can look at grace in comparison to our sin and conclude that it is truly amazing, because it "saved a wretch like me." That's the human perspective. Now he asks us to look at grace from God's perspective—to think of it as "God acting like Himself." In other words, when God acts in grace—with goodness, kindness and mercy, and with no shade of malice or resentment—God is just acting like Himself.

When Tozer asks us to see things from God's perspective, we have to realize that we cannot begin to understand His nature; much of it we have to take on faith. We are made up of "parts," but God is unified, so that all His attributes are integrated into one personality. We are finite and He is infinite. And, finally, we are fallen, and He is holy.

So when we hear someone declare something such as "God is too good to punish people," we have to recognize that it is false sentimentality, because it views God from a finite, human perspective. God's justice brings under judgment the sinner who has turned his back on God's grace, but God, being perfect, infinite and holy, can justly judge that unrepentant sinner—and do it without any trace of resentment or meanness. Even in judgment, He is still a God of grace.

Can you picture that? If not, simply take it on faith. But I think I can picture a human judge who is loving, kind and merciful, but who must condemn the unrepentant lawbreaker. In fact, wouldn't a judge who is good and kind be better able to *justly* judge the lawbreaker?

Grace Is Released at the Cross

To know God's immeasurable grace, Tozer says, we must "step under the shadow of the cross" (p. 108). Quoting John 14:6, which says that no one comes to the Father but through Jesus, and Acts 4:12, which says that there is no other name by which we can be saved, Tozer concludes that the cross is where God's grace is released. Just as the prophets who predicted the atonement didn't know quite what they were talking about, and the angels desired to look into these things further (1 Peter 1:10-12), we do not fully understand the nature of the atonement.

Tozer complains that some preachers are guilty of "vulgarizing" and "commercializing" the atonement by simplistically describing Christ's death on the cross as "paying a price" (p. 109). Tozer is not rejecting this description; I believe he is merely rejecting the idea that it fully explains the atonement. Some believers like to have everything in a neat little box; they are uncomfortable with the idea of mystery. In *Whatever Happened to Worship?*, Tozer addresses this very problem:

> There are those who pretend to know everything about God—who pretend they can explain everything about God, about His creation, about His thoughts and about His judgments. They have joined the ranks of the evangelical rationalists. They end up taking the mystery out of life and the mystery out of worship. When they have done that, they have taken God out as well.
>
> The kind of "know-it-all" attitude about God that we see in some teachers today leaves them in a very difficult position. They must roundly criticize and condemn any other man taking any position slightly different from theirs.
>
> Our cleverness and glibness and fluency may well betray our lack of that divine awe upon our spirits, silent and wonderful, that breathes a whisper, "Oh, Lord GOD, Thou knowest."

Some Things We Do Not Know

Even as deep a thinker and as profound a theologian as the Apostle Paul said, "Great is the mystery of godliness" (1 Timothy 3:16). Can't we live with a little mystery? God is infinite, so how can we expect to fully understand Him, anyway?

So don't try to understand, Tozer counsels us. Simply stand in awe at what God has done. We know the Son of God died and rose again for us. "But why? God has shut up this secret in His own great heart forever. And we can only say, 'Worthy is the Lamb' " (p. 111).

Only Believe

As a student in theology classes, I found that every attempt to develop a comprehensive "theory of the atonement" fell short, even though some theories were solidly biblical in their foundation. It is not that these theories are without some value; it is simply that, like Tozer's example of the two-year-old who asks, "Why am I here?" we must recognize that some things are beyond our ability to comprehend. "For what is of earth He lets us know, but what is of heaven, He holds in His own great heart" (p. 112).

Tozer then takes us to the parable of the prodigal son (Luke 15:11-24), the ultimate story of grace. One point he makes is that the son in the story had to change—he had to repent—in order to return to his father. But when he went back, he found that his father had *not* changed. He was still the same gracious, merciful and loving father he had always known.

His second point is made in the interpretation of the parable. The prodigal does not entirely fit the image of a sinner who comes to God for the first time, nor of a backslider who comes back to God. The reason? He represents both—in fact, he represents the whole human race. We went out to the pigsty in Adam, and we came back in Christ.

Where the Grace Is

Putting those two points together, Tozer concludes that if we are out of God's grace, we need to return. We can only return in Christ, because that's where God's grace is. If we try any other way besides Christ, we aren't returning. We're still in the pigsty. "If you set your teeth against Him, the grace of God might as well not exist for you" (p. 115). But if we return in Christ, we find that all of God's nature is on our side—even His justice (1 John 1:9).

Tozer's concluding prayer, that God would sweep away all our self-righteousness, is one that bears repeating. It seems to be a recurring theme for many of us that the weed of self-righteousness has to be continually rooted out from the garden of our hearts. Spend some time searching your heart for weeds to pull. Ask God to give you a fresh awareness that your new life in Christ is by grace alone.

LESSON PLAN—Group Study

AIM: That my students would have a fresh understanding of God's grace, especially in their own lives.

Introduction

1. Open in prayer.

2. Have someone read the eight Scripture passages at the beginning of the chapter (Genesis 6:8; Exodus 33:17; Proverbs 3:34; John 1:16-17; Romans 3:24; Romans 5:15; Ephesians 1:6-7; 1 Peter 5:10). List on the board different aspects of grace that the group can derive from these passages.

Grace Flows from God's Goodness

1. Ask the class to explain the difference between mercy and grace. Refer to the comments in the personal study and/or in the subsection of the chapter, if necessary.

2. Read John 1:17. Ask what the typical teaching about this verse is, which Tozer disproves. If necessary, read Exodus 33:13, 17 to refute the popular idea that "Moses knew only law."

Grace: The Only Means of Salvation

Ask how the Old Testament believers were saved. On what basis were they saved? (On the basis of grace, of course! What do you think this chapter is about?) Read Revelation 13:8 and point out that God's view of time is different than ours, so that Old Testament believers could "look ahead" to the perfect sacrifice of Christ.

Grace Is What God Is Like

Read the excerpt from *The Root of the Righteous* in the personal study (*Study Guide*, p. 56). Ask the group if this changes their view of God. Does it affect the way they relate to God?

How to Look at Grace

Have the class discuss the statement, "God is too good to punish anyone." What is the error in this line of reasoning?

Grace Is Released at the Cross

Tozer says that describing Christ's death on the cross as merely "paying a price" is "vulgarizing the atonement." What does he mean by that?

Some Things We Do Not Know

Read First Timothy 3:16. Ask the group what a "mystery" is [something we do not know, cannot explain or understand]. Why is it hard for North Americans in the twenty-first century to live with mystery?

Only Believe

Read Luke 15:11-24. What aspects of God's grace are portrayed in this story?

Where the Grace Is

Ask how the prodigal son was able to appropriate grace [by returning to his father]. How do we appropriate God's grace in our lives?

Closing

1. Ask the group to close their eyes as you read Tozer's concluding prayer (p. 115).

2. Assign chapter 7 to read for next week's class.

3. Close in prayer.

Chapter 7:
God's Omnipresence

Personal Study

Supplementary Materials: A.W. Tozer, *God Tells the
Man Who Cares* (Camp Hill, PA: WingSpread
Publishers, 1992); C.S. Lewis, *The Great Divorce*
(New York: Macmillan, 1946); A.W. Tozer, *The
Knowledge of the Holy* (San Francisco: Harper and
Row, 1961).

I n previous chapters, we've looked at such things
as mercy and grace—attributes of God that we
can relate to and even emulate, to some limited ex-
tent. We can be merciful and gracious, and thereby
be "children of [our] Father which is in heaven"
(Matthew 5:45). But with omnipresence, we return
to an attribute which we *cannot* share with God. We
cannot understand it as well because it is a function
of His infinite being, and we are finite creatures.

As with other chapters, Tozer begins with several
Scriptures, but here he gives a most unexpected explanation as to why. I assumed he would say that
these verses are given to prove the biblical basis of

the doctrine of God's omnipresence. Instead, these are given to show that "the Holy Scriptures have their origin in the nature of God" (p. 118). What an interesting reversal of thought!

What Omnipresence Is

Tozer establishes at least three aspects of God's omnipresence: God is near to everywhere, everyone and everything; God has no borders; and God has no size. The first aspect is the traditional definition of omnipresence; when we hear it, we nod our heads and say we understand. The other two aspects—that God has no borders and no size—may seem strange to our ears, because we have never thought through the implications of the first aspect.

If God is everywhere, then He could not have any borders, because a border indicates the point at which something *ends*. Since God does not end, but is infinite, He cannot have borders. And God cannot have size, because size indicates that something is *measurable*. If God is infinite, He cannot be measured. (You may recall this same discussion in the chapter on God's infinitude.)

This is not just semantics; Tozer is trying to clear our minds of our little picture of God: "We think rightly about God and spiritual things only when we rule out the concept of space altogether" (p. 119). Jeremiah 23:24 tells us that God fills heaven and earth. I like how Tozer compares this to the way the ocean "fills" a bucket—but there's still a lot of ocean left! "The heaven and heaven of heavens cannot contain him" (2 Chronicles 2:6).

It's important for us to stretch our minds around these thoughts, so that we can see our error in thinking of God as being "far away, beyond the starlit sky" (p. 120). In *God Tells the Man Who Cares*, Tozer addresses this attitude with wry humor:

> The Bible teaches plainly enough the doctrine of the divine omnipresence, but for the masses of professed Christians this is the era of the Absentee God. Most Christians speak of God in the manner usually reserved for a departed loved one. . . .
>
> Surely God would not have created us to be satisfied with nothing less than His presence if He had intended that we should get on with nothing more than His absence.

So why do we think of God as remote?

Our Remoteness from God

In the realm of the spirit, distance is irrelevant. Jesus can be in heaven and still be with us always (Matthew 28:20). So if we feel distant from God, Tozer reminds us, there is a different cause. "But we are shut off from God . . . because there is a dissimilarity in nature" (p. 121). He illustrates this "dissimilarity in nature" by asking us to imagine an angel and an ape in the same room. Because their natures are so different, they cannot have communion or compatibility.

God is always *right here*. So why do we think of Him as far away? Because our sin makes us unlike Him in our moral nature. In Ephesians 2:1-3 and 4:17-19, there is a word that identifies this "far away" feeling: *alienation.* Like a very godly man and an evil, sinful man who sit together on a train have little common ground to carry on a conversation, we have no common ground with God when we are still in sin.

We feel alienated from God because He speaks the language of the spirit, while we speak the language of the flesh. God lives in a culture of holiness, while we live in a culture of sin. God is near, but so far away in nature.

Paul describes mankind's search for God in this way: "That they should seek the Lord, if haply they might feel after him, and find him" (Acts 17:27). It sounds like a blind man groping around an unfamiliar room, or like a man who doesn't know the language trying to communicate with signs.

Illustrations from Scripture

Our remoteness from God reminds me of the wife who complained to her husband, "We don't sit close together in the car anymore." He replied, "Honey, I'm sitting behind the steering wheel; if we don't sit as close as we used to, I'm not the one who's moved!"

In fact, it is we who put the "distance" between ourselves and God, because we cannot stand the dissimilarity in our moral natures. Tozer illustrates this with examples from Scripture: Adam hid in the garden when he sinned (Genesis 3:8); Jonah tried to run away from God when he refused to do what God wanted (Jonah 1:3); Peter begged Jesus to get away from him, "for I am a sinful man" (Luke 5:8). "It is

the heart that puts distance between us and God"
(pp. 126-127).

The Bliss of Moral Creatures

There is an opposite experience from this sense of
alienation. It is the pure bliss of His manifest presence. This could be the most important point Tozer
makes in this chapter: There is a difference—a vast
difference—between God's presence (which is everywhere) and His *manifest* presence (when He reveals
Himself to man). His manifest presence is the exclu-
sive experience of those moral creatures who allow
Him to change them to His likeness. This is why
First John 3:2 tells us that in heaven we shall be like
Him.

As Tozer puts it, His manifest presence is what
makes heaven heaven, and the lack of it is what
makes hell hell. In *The Great Divorce*, C.S. Lewis'
allegory about a bus trip from hell to heaven, the res-
idents of hell find they cannot enjoy heaven because
it is not made for them. This is what Tozer is talking
about. Sinful men cannot experience God's manifest
presence because they are so morally dissimilar. So
how, Tozer asks, can sinful men ever come near to
God?

The Reconciliation of the Dissimilar

For an answer to this question, Tozer turns to the
Old Testament character Jacob. If any man was unlike God in his moral nature, it was the deceiver and
conniver Jacob, whose very name (meaning "supplanter") betrays his aggressive, grasping nature. Yet

this is the same man who said, "Surely the LORD is in this place; and I knew it not" (Genesis 28:16), which indicated that he had begun to sense God's manifest presence. How did this happen?

After first establishing that man cannot change himself to become like God, Tozer concludes that there must be *reconciliation* between God and man. Thank God that is what happened in Christ (2 Corinthians 5:19). But how?

One way two parties are reconciled is through *compromise*. The problem here, however, is that this is not simply a difference of *opinion* between God and man, but a difference of *nature* between God and man. Can God and man each come halfway? Of course not! How can God say, "Well, you be a little more holy and I'll be a little more sinful, and we'll meet in between"? It is not because God is stubborn; it's because God is God. How can God be anything less than perfectly holy and righteous? If we have learned anything from these studies on God's attributes, we have at least learned that!

Ironically, God solved this problem not by coming halfway, but coming all the way! God became man in the person of Jesus Christ, but He did not compromise His holy nature. And Jesus died on the cross for our sin, reconciling us to God and giving us a chance to come all the way too. We can become "partakers of the divine nature" (2 Peter 1:4). Tozer explains: "It means that when the sinner comes home, repents and believes on Christ savingly, God implants in the heart of that previous sinner some of His own nature" (p. 132).

Tozer returns to the "ape and angel" illustration to point out that

> If the great God Almighty would deposit the glorious celestial nature of the angel in the ape, the ape would leap to his feet and shake hands with the angel and call him by name, because similarity would instantly be there. (pp. 132-133)

That is why Jacob could say, "Surely the LORD is in this place; and I knew it not" (Genesis 28:16). Tozer notes that Jacob says, "the LORD *is* in this place" (present tense), and "I *knew* it not" (past tense). God was there all the time, but a change came over Jacob—he was converted—and suddenly, he knew what he had never known before: the manifest presence of God.

Communion with God

This, Tozer says, is why new converts are so happy: The *conscious* presence of God has been restored to them. God's conscious presence is what makes heaven heaven, and the absence of His conscious presence is what makes hell hell. If we have truly come to faith in Christ, our spirit joins with His Spirit, we partake of His nature and bask in the presence of God.

Is Tozer saying the born-again Christian should *always* be deliriously happy? Not at all. In his book *The Knowledge of the Holy*, Tozer notes that a child may cry even in the safety and protection of its mother's arms. Similarly, the manifest presence of God does not shield us from all of life's pain. But the sense of alienation, the loneliness of separation from God, is gone forever—if we know Christ.

LESSON PLAN—Group Study

AIM: That my students would have a new appreciation and awareness of God's presence in their lives.

Introduction

1. Open in prayer.

2. Have someone read the five Scripture passages at the beginning of the chapter (1 Kings 8:27; Jeremiah 23:23; Acts 17:27-28; Psalm 16:8; Psalm 139:7-10).

What Omnipresence Is

1. Ask the class to define omnipresence. What makes this attribute more difficult for us to comprehend than those we have most recently studied, such as God's mercy, grace and justice? (It is an attribute we cannot share with Him, because we are finite creatures.)

2. Discuss what Tozer means when he says that God has no borders and no size.

Our Remoteness from God

1. If God is everywhere, why do people often speak of Him as far away? Tozer blames it on "a dissimilarity of moral nature." What does he mean by that? Discuss.

2. Ask if anyone has spent time in a foreign country, interacting with people of a different culture. Invite them to share what it felt like to be "different" from everyone else (or, if you have had such an experience, share your own feelings of alienation). Then read Acts 17:27 and discuss how living in a foreign culture is similar to Paul's description of mankind's search for God.

Illustrations from Scripture

Present the examples of Adam after he sinned (he hid himself), Jonah after God spoke to him (he ran away), and Peter after he witnessed one of Jesus' early miracles (he asked the Lord to get away from him). Why is this our natural reaction to the presence of God?

The Bliss of Moral Creatures

What is the *manifest* presence of God? What is the prerequisite to experiencing God's manifest presence? Read First John 3:2 to present or confirm the answer to these questions.

The Reconciliation of the Dissimilar

1. Discuss how Tozer would respond to the question, "Why can't God strike a compromise—just overlook our differences and let us into heaven?" (The fallacy of that question is the theme of C.S. Lewis' *The Great Divorce*.)

2. Read Second Peter 1:4. Discuss the implications of being "partakers of the divine nature." (Don't

allow the class to pass over this with pat "Sunday school" answers. Get them to grapple with the wonder of having the infinite Creator dwelling inside them.)

Communion with God

If we have come to faith in Christ and can experience the conscious, manifest presence of God, why don't we live in constant bliss? (Because we still live in a fallen world, and have many of the same needs and troubles as the rest of the world. The difference is our constant communion with God, which helps us face the worst that life can dish out.)

Closing

1. Ask the class to close their eyes and meditate on the presence of God. After a moment of silence, invite anyone to raise their hand if they would like to experience a deeper measure of God's manifest presence in their life.

2. Assign chapter 8 to read for next week's class.

3. Close in prayer, especially remembering those who have raised their hands.

Chapter 8:
God's Immanence

Personal Study

Supplementary Materials: A.B. Simpson, *Loving as Jesus Loves* (Camp Hill, PA: WingSpread Publishers, 1996).

A s with all the chapters in this book, Tozer is presenting far more than a dry, doctrinal treatise on a certain attribute of God. Instead, he is trying to relate how this attribute affects our personal relationship with God. At first it may appear that Tozer is covering much the same ground with immanence that he did with omnipresence in the previous chapter. And it is true that *omnipresence* (God is everywhere) is very closely related to *immanence* (God penetrates everything). "God dwells in His universe and yet the universe dwells in God" (p. 138).

However, the previous chapter is addressed to the non-Christian, essentially. Believers can relate to the message of the chapter (the feeling of God being far away), but only as they see that it tells them what they *were* like, not the way they are now (or should be, at least). In this chapter, Tozer frankly admits that most Christians (and he includes himself) still feel a sense of

75

remoteness from God. Why this is, and what can be done about it, is the thrust of this message.

Tozer begins by introducing the three divine acts that bring us salvation: atonement, justification and regeneration. Of these three, only regeneration is subjective, occurring in the heart, causing us to be "partakers of the divine nature" (2 Peter 1:4).

Restoration of Moral Comparability

A regenerated person, having partaken of the divine nature, has a moral comparability, or compatibility, to God. Our moral likeness to God "allows God to draw feelingly near to a person" (p. 141). There can be no communion between two beings that are completely unlike each other. And God, says Tozer, is "violently unlike" the sinner. But if we are regenerated, we can "put on the new man" (Colossians 3:10), which has a likeness to God, a "family resemblance."

So far Tozer is not saying much that is different from the previous chapter. But at this point, he breaks new ground when he asks the question, "Why then this serious problem among real Christians— this feeling that God is far away or that we are far away from God?" (p. 142).

At this point, the reader who was expecting a theological treatise on the immanence of God is likely to feel that Tozer is straying off the subject. But actually he is just one step ahead of these readers in his thinking. He has already defined the immanence of God; now he is applying it to our relationship with Him.

If God's presence penetrates and permeates the universe, if "in him we live, and move, and have our being" (Acts 17:28), why don't we sense His pervasive presence at every moment? Why are we like a man who starves to death while seated before a banquet? Certainly, the unbeliever may not sense God's presence, but we who have been born again, who are children of God, why do we feel so remote?

One school of thought on this is that we must simply take it on faith, to rejoice in God's presence even if we don't "feel" it. There is some truth to this, and Tozer himself has warned elsewhere in his writings that we should not *live* by feelings. And who would want to argue against faith? But living by faith does not mean we should completely ignore our feelings. Sometimes a feeling, such as a sense of being far from God, is a signal that something is wrong.

When all is said and done, if we claim to be rejoicing in God's presence when we still feel a remoteness, we're just kidding ourselves. As Tozer puts it,

> To know something in your head is one thing; to feel it in your heart is another. And I think most Christians are trying to be happy without having a sense of the Presence. It's like trying to have a bright day without having the sun. (p. 143)

Yearning for God

These believers who try to live without a conscious, manifest presence of God in their lives are referred to by Tozer as "theological Christians" (p. 143). They understand they are saved and they have all the facts straight—and there's nothing wrong with that. But deep inside there is a yearning for God, no matter how much they want to deny it. It comes out in prayers such as, "Lord, come and show Thyself to us," or in hymns such as "Draw Me Nearer."

This yearning for God is really a good thing, Tozer declares:

> This desire, this yearning to be near to God is, in fact, a yearning to be like Him. It's the yearning of the ransomed heart to be like God so there can be perfect communion, so the heart and God can come together in a fellowship that is divine. (p. 145)

In *The Pursuit of God*, Tozer expands on this theme:

> To have found God and still to pursue Him is the soul's paradox of love, scorned indeed by the too-easily-satisfied religionist, but justified in happy experience by the children of the burning heart. . . . Come near to the holy men and women of the past and you will soon feel the heat of their desire after God. They mourned for Him, they prayed and wrestled and sought for Him day and night, in season and out, and when they had found Him the finding was all the sweeter for the long seeking.

What we are yearning for is a *manifestation* of God's presence—a yearning we should *cultivate*, not ignore. This desire to be *near* God is a yearning to be *like* God. But how do we know what God is like, so that we can know where we fall short? Tozer has a simple answer: God is like Christ!

The Holiness of Christ

One quality of Jesus, for example, is holiness. But we become stained and spotted by the world, Tozer says, and we allow months, even years, to pass without repentance. This reminds me of something I once heard Fred Hartley say in a sermon: "I know I've repented of my sins—because I'm still repenting!" Repentance is not a one-time act; it's a way of life, an abiding attitude of the heart.

A carnal Christian may be regenerated but still have unholy feelings, desires and motivations. How can a holy God commune with such carnality? These things keep us from experiencing God's manifest presence, just as heavy clouds obscure the sun. We need to repent.

The Unselfishness of Christ

Jesus is also unselfish. He gave Himself for us. Yet so many Christians are self-centered and self-indulgent. Tozer has a good way to test this area of your life: "You'll know you're self-centered if anybody crosses you and your hackles go up" (p. 147). How true—and how frequently true of myself and others!

Our self-indulgence is evident in what we spend our time and money on. What do our spending habits, for example, say about our desires, our priorities? Can a selfless Christ commune with a self-centered, self-indulgent Christian? I wonder whether someone who is wrapped up in self can have much communion with anyone at all.

The Love of Christ

Closely related to selflessness is love. Christ loved us so much that He gave His all, holding nothing

79

back. Tozer complains that, in contrast, too many Christians are "cheap" with God: "We put our spiritual life on a budget" (p. 148). But "Christ pleased not himself" (Romans 15:3).

Some might question how our lack of love and selflessness can keep God from communion with us. But we need to realize that it is we who are blocking the way, not God. For proof, Tozer refers to Song of Solomon 5:2-6. The bridegroom (Christ) wants his bride to join him. But she does not want to leave her bed. By the time she tears herself away, he has left. They have no fellowship together because she is so selfish. In the latter part of the chapter, the bride is yearning for his return.

A.B. Simpson comments on this passage in his devotional study of the Song of Solomon, *Loving as Jesus Loves*:

> The causes of the beloved woman's failure were indolence and self-indulgence. This was a great slight to her lord. She had preferred her comfort to his. She could lie in luxurious ease while he was standing outside the door, his head wet with the dew. . . . What a sad, sad symbol of the Lord Jesus Christ with respect to the very church that He has redeemed and wedded to Himself. She in luxury and selfishness, and He out in the cold and the darkness.

Other Qualities of Christ

There are other qualities of Christ that are in such great contrast to what is so often seen in our lives. He is kind, yet we are so often harsh. He forgave those who tortured Him, yet we can be so petty and vengeful. He is zealous, when we are often luke-warm. And imagine how distant the humble Christ feels among us when we act so proud and arrogant!

Are you feeling convicted yet? I know I am! Tozer was preaching this at least forty years ago; how could he know what I am like today? The truth is, there's not much originality in sin!

Likeness Is Not Justification

Does all of this mean we are not saved? Not at all. Tozer reminds us that justification is not the same as likeness to God. By Christ's death on the cross, we are regenerated, so that the seed of new life is planted in us. "But regeneration does not perfect the image of God in you" (p. 152). The seed has to grow. Tozer compares this to an artist with a painting. First, he puts general outlines on the canvas and adds shading, until the image gradually appears and the details are filled in.

Our dissimilarity holds us back from experiencing the manifest presence of God. The only solution is to repent of our unlikeness. Tozer compares it to Peter, who, just before he denied the Lord, "followed him afar off" (Matthew 26:58). But upon his denial, he realized how far he was from his Lord, and "wept bitterly" (26:75).

The said truth is that many of us are comfortable in this condition—we've gotten used to following the Lord "afar off." It's a pathetic way to live. We need to seriously consider Tozer's plaintive question, "Have you any tears for your unlikeness?" (p. 154).

LESSON PLAN—*Group Study*

AIM: To help my students understand the difference between God's presence and His *manifest* presence, and to encourage them to grow in their desire to commune with God.

Introduction

1. Open in prayer.

2. Have someone read the Scripture passages at the beginning of the chapter (1 Kings 8:27; Acts 17:27-28; Psalm 139:7-10).

3. Begin by asking the group to define *immanence*. How does it differ from *omnipresence*?

4. While we know God is always near, our sense of His presence can vary. Ask the students to draw a chart (hand out paper and pencils if necessary), showing how close they felt to God over the past week. (The chart is for the individual's own reference; it should not be shared with the rest of the class.)

Restoration of Moral Comparability

1. Read Colossians 3:10. Discuss what it means to "put on the new man."

2. As Christians we are to live by faith, not by feelings. Yet Tozer tells us we should pay attention to the "feeling" of remoteness from God. Is this contradictory? How do we do both? Discuss.

Yearning for God

1. Read the quote from *The Pursuit of God* in the personal study section (*Study Guide*, p. 78). Ask how this relates to our feelings of remoteness from God.

2. What standard should we use to measure our likeness to God? [Christ]

The Holiness of Christ

Tozer asks, "Is it possible to be a Christian and be unholy?" (p. 147). Discuss.

The Unselfishness of Christ

Ask for responses to this comment from the personal study: "Our self-indulgence is evident in what we spend our time and money on. What do our spending habits, for example, say about our desires, our priorities?" (*Study Guide*, p. 79).

The Love of Christ

1. What does Tozer mean when he says, "We put our spiritual life on a budget" (p. 148)?

2. Read Song of Solomon 5:2-6. Ask what the attitude is of the bride in verse 3; in verse 4; and in verse 6. Point out that the hopeless tone of this verse ("I called him, but he gave me no answer") is not the end of the story—and does not have to be the end of our story, either!

Other Qualities of Christ

List on a board the four attributes of Christ that Tozer mentions in this section: kindness, forgiveness, zeal and humility. Ask the class to suggest specific actions in their daily lives that would change if they were more like Christ in these areas. (Examples might be acting more politely to family and friends, being more diligent in daily devotions, etc.)

Likeness Is Not Justification

1. What is the difference between being regenerated and being like Christ?

2. Why do we "get used to" being remote from God? What can we do to get out of that rut?

Closing

1. Before praying, invite anyone who is convicted about their unlikeness to God to raise their hand as an expression of repentance. (Don't ask the class to close their eyes; repentance should be a public thing.)

2. Assign chapter 9 to read for next week's class.

3. Close in prayer, remembering those who have raised their hands.

Chapter 9:
God's Holiness

Personal Study

Supplementary Materials: Jonathan Edwards, "A Treatise Concerning Religious Affections," in *The Works of Jonathan Edwards*, Vol. 2, ed. Perry Miller (New Haven: Yale Univ. Press, 1957); A.W. Tozer, *Worship: The Missing Jewel* (Camp Hill, PA: WingSpread Publishers, 1992).

If there is one attribute of God that stands above all others, it has to be holiness. Jonathan Edwards said, "A true love of God must begin with a delight in His holiness, and not with a delight in any other attribute; for no other attribute is truly lovely without this." And yet, how do we develop a "delight" in holiness? It is "foreign soil" for us fallen, sinful creatures. Tozer found it difficult to preach about, because he sensed that he could never do it justice.

We Cannot Understand Holiness

There's a dual difficulty in understanding God's holiness. Along with the intellectual challenge of understanding an infinite God, we also must wrestle with our own sense of vileness as we contemplate an infinitely holy God. We were made to be holy like our Creator, but "we are fallen beings—spiritually, morally, mentally and physically. We are fallen in all the ways that man can fall" (p. 158). And every aspect of society is fallen along with us.

If we are fallen beings in a fallen world, how can we understand God's holiness? Does a fish know that it is wet? "This kind of world," Tozer explains, "gets into our pores, into our nerves, until we have lost the ability to conceive of the holy" (p. 159). Even our words (purity, moral excellence, rectitude, honor, truth, righteousness) seem inadequate to describe it.

The Scriptures use suggestion and association to describe God's holiness, Tozer says, because language is inadequate. Read Exodus 19 and look for manifestations of God that suggest or are associated with His holiness.

Two Words for Holiness

As Tozer points out, there are two main words for "holy" in the Old Testament—one that usually stands for God and is often translated "the Holy One," and one that is usually used to describe created things (including humans) and means "holy by contact or association (with God)." These two words seem to suggest that God can impart His holiness onto His people.

In the New Testament, the word for holiness literally means "an awful [awe-full] thing." This, Tozer says, is where we have fallen short today. Under the influence of humanistic teaching, we are too "familiar" with God; we have lost a sense of His majestic holiness, His "awful, unapproachable quality" (p. 164). Yes, believe it or not, this is coming from the same Tozer that elsewhere calls on us to approach God in intimacy, as a little child. Is he being contradictory? Not at all. In *Worship: The Missing Jewel*, Tozer explains this apparent paradox:

> Worship, I say, rises or falls with our concept of God; that is why I do not believe in these half-converted cowboys who call God "the Man Upstairs." I do not think they worship at all because their concept of God is unworthy of God and unworthy of them. And if there is one terrible disease in the Church of Christ, it is that we do not see God as great as He is. We're too familiar with God.
>
> Communion with God is one thing; familiarity with God is quite another thing.

The Fiery Holiness of God

The concept of the presence of God as a "devouring fire" and "everlasting burnings" (Isaiah 33:14) is, I must confess, an overwhelming thought to me. I suppose, however, it is intended to be. By citing various Scripture passages that portray God as fire, Tozer is trying to help us see beyond the flippant attitude that so many have toward God today. We lack an awesome, awe-full respect for His holy majesty.

We are not alone. The Lord chided the people of Israel, saying, "thou thoughtest that I was altogether such an one as thyself" (Psalm 50:21). C.S. Lewis echoes Tozer's point in a comment in *Mere Christianity*:

> God is the only comfort, He is also the supreme terror. . . . Some people talk as if meeting the gaze of absolute goodness would be fun. They need to think again. They are only playing with religion.

How can we who wish to draw nearer to God approach the unapproachable flame? There is a solution, Tozer tells us. If you put a piece of iron in a fire, "the iron can learn to live with the fire by absorbing the fire and beginning to glow" (p. 166). This is a common illustration used by the medieval devotional writers to explain the work of the Holy Spirit in the believer—and again, another suggestion that God can impart His holiness unto His people.

Tozer's idea of "the fiery holiness of God" and His unapproachable majesty can be easily misunderstood. We may misinterpret it and think that God is too "dangerous" to approach, so we shouldn't try. The real truth is that God wants us to approach Him—but we can't expect to come out of the confrontation unscathed! Remember how Jacob came away from it with a chronic limp? The good news is that the only thing that really dies is our sin and selfishness. Like C.S. Lewis said in *The Lion, the Witch and the Wardrobe*, "He's not a tame Lion—but He's good"!

The Holy One and the Sinner

Tozer then sets his sights now on the presumptuous sinner, who thinks he can decide *when* he will turn to God, or who turns to God only to get something from Him. We need to realize just Whom we are dealing with when we approach God. If we had a better picture of His awesome holiness, we would not neglect to repent of those "hanging-on" sins. We would not insult His majesty by coming to Him in prayer with a "shopping list." He is the God who is "of purer eyes than to behold evil, and canst not look on iniquity" (Habakkuk 1:13), and "It is of the LORD's mercies that we are not consumed" (Lamentations 3:22).

The crowning Scripture that Tozer directs our attention to is Hebrews 12:14: "Follow . . . holiness, without which no man shall see the Lord." He charges the modern believer with not taking this verse seriously, because we try to reinterpret it to mean something else. We also excuse ourselves by saying that God "knows we are but dust."

Tozer isn't buying it, and neither should we. We worship a God who is too pure to look on sin, the awesome Holy One. And He has told us to be holy as He is holy (Leviticus 11:45; 1 Peter 1:16). A true vision of His holiness should cause us to live lives of repentance that we may never have anything between us and the Holy One of Israel.

LESSON PLAN—Group Study

AIM: To help my students catch a vision of God's awesome holiness, and realize our need to live holy lives as well.

Introduction

1. Open in prayer.

2. Have someone read the six Scripture passages at
   the beginning of the chapter (Exodus 15:11; Job
   15:15, 25:5-6; Psalm 22:3; Proverbs 9:10; Isaiah
   6:3).

We Cannot Understand Holiness

Ask for volunteers to venture a definition of holiness. Then read the last paragraph on page 159 of
the book. Why is it hard for us to understand holiness?

Two Words for Holiness

1. Explain that there are two main words for "holy"
   in the Old Testament: one that usually describes
   God, and another that usually means "holy by
   association." Discuss what that means for us in
   our relationship to God.

2. Discuss what Tozer means when he says that
   many Christians are too "familiar" with God.
   Are we guilty of that today? How does this mesh
   with previous statements by Tozer that call for
   us to draw near to God in intimate relationship?

The Fiery Holiness of God

1. Discuss the picture Tozer presents of God as
   fire. How can we see God as a "devouring fire"
   and still draw near? How can we see Him as
   "the supreme terror," as C.S. Lewis puts it, and
   still desire Him?

2. Read the last paragraph on page 166 in the book about "the iron in the fire" and discuss how that illustrates the work of the Holy Spirit in a person's life.

The Holy One and the Sinner

Have different class members read the following Scriptures, in this order: Habakkuk 1:13; Lamentations 3:22; Hebrews 12:14; First Peter 1:15-16. How do these verses relate to our daily Christian walk? What do they say about our daily priorities?

Closing

1. Have the class join together in the prayer at the end of the chapter (pp. 174-175).

2. Assign chapter 10 to read for next week's class.

3. Close in prayer.

Chapter 10:
God's Perfection

Personal Study

Supplementary Materials: Stanley Grenz and Roger Olson, *Who Needs Theology?* (Downers Grove, IL: InterVarsity Press, 1996); Larry Dixon, *Heaven: Thinking Now about Forever* (2002).

Tozer begins this message by quoting a single verse (Psalm 50:2) and pointing out the three prominent words in the passage: perfection, beauty and God. From there he quickly launches into a critique of evangelical Christianity over the past fifty years. This abrupt change of subject may bother some readers; what, after all, does this have to do with God's perfection? But be patient; Tozer will show how this relates to the main topic in due time.

As you read what Tozer has to say about "our gains and losses," remember that he is speaking in the mid-1950s, so for him, "the past fifty years" is the first half of the twentieth century. As twenty-first-century Christians, we need to decide if his critique applies to our recent past as well.

Our Gains and Losses

Tozer identifies several positive gains that evangelicals have enjoyed, including increased church attendance, more people identifying themselves as Christians, an increase in the number of schools, colleges and seminaries, dramatic growth in Christian literature, an increase in the popularity of the gospel, better communication and great strides in worldwide evangelism. "We cannot deny," he admits, "that a lot of good is being done and the gospel is being spread around" (p. 178). However, he adds, we have had a loss in "religious fear," leading to "flippancy and familiarity."

No Awareness of the Eternal

Tozer also identifies a loss in the Church of an awareness of the invisible and eternal, a consciousness of the divine presence and divine majesty. He echoes much the same thing when describing the average evangelical church service in *God Tells the Man Who Cares*:

> In the majority of our meetings, there is scarcely a trace of reverent thought, no recognition of the unity of the body, little sense of the divine Presence, no moment of stillness, no solemnity, no wonder, no holy fear. But so often there is a dull or a breezy song leader full of awkward jokes, as well as a chairman announcing each "number" with the old radio continuity patter in an effort to make everything hang together.

True worship—in fact, the essence of Christianity—is defined by Tozer as a believer's "ability to withdraw inwardly and commune in the secret place with God in the shrine of his own hidden spirit" (p. 181). We have almost lost this ability, he says.

Now that you have heard Tozer's critique of the situation during his lifetime, what do you think? Would it accurately describe *our* gains and losses over the past few decades? I venture to suggest that it would, because Tozer is identifying here a cycle that the Church seems to continually slip into.

External Gains, Internal Losses

The cycle can be defined as this: When our gains are mostly external, we start to have losses that are internal. Tozer is not saying that our external gains have *caused* our internal losses, but that it is possible to focus on the externals *to the neglect of* our inner relationship with God. The cause of our losses is deeper—it is a lack of recognition of who God is. "I believe that we never can recover our glory," Tozer contends, "until we are brought to see again the awful [awe-full] perfections of God" (p. 181).

Didn't I tell you? It may take him a while, but eventually Tozer comes back around to the main topic—in this case, God's perfection. At this point, Tozer begins discussing the attribute of perfection, but he starts by addressing an apparent contradiction between perfection and infinitude.

What Is Perfection?

If perfection is defined as "the highest possible degree of excellence" (p. 182), how can this apply to God, if nothing is *im*possible for Him? Perfect means to have everything you are supposed to have (a baby is "perfect" if it has two arms, two legs, ten fingers, ten toes, etc.) and nothing it's not supposed to have (no *extra* fingers or toes!). But how can we apply that to God, who is infinite?

We think of perfect as an *absolute* word, and we conclude that "nobody's perfect, except for God." But the Bible uses perfect as a *relative* word, to compare one creature to another. God is not a creature and He cannot be compared to anyone or anything. So why does the Bible use the word "perfect" to refer to God—as well as to created things? It sounds as if Tozer is painting himself into a corner with this argument!

No Degrees in God

If you recall what Tozer said in the chapter on God's infinitude about there being "no degrees in God," this should begin to make some sense. We can't say (strictly speaking) that God is "excellent," because if something excels, it is in comparison to other things, and God is not to be compared to finite creatures. "To whom then will ye liken me?" (Isaiah 40:25). God is *incomparable*. Tozer suggests that this may be the source for the commandment against graven images in Exodus 20:4.

Despite all this, Jesus used the *same word* for perfect for both God and us when He said we should be perfect as our Father in heaven (Matthew 5:48). Why? Tozer says it is the limitations of human language and thought that prevent us from conceiving of God's unqualified fullness and completeness.

When we say a human is perfect, we mean they do the best a human can do. But when we say God is perfect, there is no qualification.

Here Tozer returns to the Scripture passage he began with: "Out of Zion, the perfection of beauty, God hath shined" (Psalm 50:2). What made Zion so perfectly beautiful? It was "the shining God who dwelt between the wings of the cherubim" (p. 187). Because the *shekinah* glory of God was there, Zion was beautiful. All things are beautiful as they move closer to God and ugly as they move farther away.

What Honors God Is Beautiful

This is what makes a hymn beautiful, though it may not be as artistically polished as some secular music—it honors God. It is what makes the Bible beautiful. It is what makes theology beautiful.

The beauty of theology, however, may be hard for some believers to see. The word "theology," for many of us, conjures up visions of skeptics in ivory towers, building massive arguments against the authority of Scripture and all true faith. But when we consider that theology, in its simplest, purest definition, is "thinking about God," we realize that everyone practices theology. (For an excellent and easy-to-read discussion of this topic, see *Who Needs Theology?*, by Stanley Grenz and Roger Olson.) Tozer defines beautiful theology this way:

> It is the mind down on its knees in a state of breathless devotion, reasoning about God—or it should be. It is possible for theology to become a very hard and aloof thing, and we can lose God

right out of our theology. But the kind of theology I'm talking about, the study of God, is a beautiful thing. (p. 188)

Heaven, Tozer adds, "is the place of supreme beauty," because "the perfection of beauty is there" (p. 189). We need to revise our ideas of heaven, Tozer says, by thinking and learning more about it. Larry Dixon, in his book, *Heaven: Thinking Now about Forever*, echoes Tozer's plea, saying that modern Christians have allowed heaven to be "stolen" from us by our preoccupation with this world.

Finally, Tozer leads us to the ultimate beauty: Christ Himself.

Beauty Centers around Christ

Beauty centers around Christ because He Himself is God, the source of all beauty. This is an internal, not external, beauty. Heaven is beautiful because Jesus is there. And on the opposite end of the scale, hell must be the ultimate in ugliness and imperfection, because it is so far from God.

This puts earth halfway between, where we see beauty and ugliness all around us. Our choice, the greatest choice we have to make, is whether we spend our lives seeking after beauty or ugliness.

Nothing Bad Is Beautiful

Anything that is bad cannot be beautiful, Tozer concludes.

It is possible for an unholy thing to be pretty or attractive, even charming. But it is not possible for it to be beautiful. Only that which is holy can be beautiful ultimately. (p. 191)

Christ came to save us from the ugliness of hell and bring us to heaven, the place of the perfection of beauty.

Nothing Wonderful in the World

That is why the world has nothing to offer us, Tozer says, because only God is beautiful and wonderful. We spend too much time and effort on mortal things, when God wants to give us His Presence.

What good is all our busy religion if God isn't in it? What good is it if we've lost majesty, reverence, worship—an awareness of the divine? What good is it if we've lost a sense of the Presence and the ability to retreat within our own hearts and meet God in the garden? If we've lost that, why build another church? Why make more converts to an effete Christianity? Why bring people to follow after a Savior so far off that He doesn't own them? (pp. 194-195)

Tozer ends this message by calling on us to improve our Christianity by raising our concept of God—which was, if you recall, his purpose in teaching about God's attributes in the first place.

If I have a low concept of God, my religion can only be a cheap, watery affair. But if my concept of God is worthy of God then it can be noble and dignified; it can be reverent, profound, beautiful. This is what I want to see once more among men. Pray that way, won't you? (p. 195)

His concluding prayer, the longest one in the book, is nothing more than a plea for revival. It would be well worth one's time to read, meditate on and pray that prayer.

LESSON PLAN—Group Study

AIM: To help my students understand God's perfection and develop a concept of God that is worthy of Him.

Introduction

1. Open in prayer.

2. Have someone read the Scripture passages at the beginning of the chapter (Exodus 15:11; Job 15:15; 25:5-6; Psalm 22:3; Proverbs 9:10; Isaiah 6:3).

3. Read Psalm 50:2 and ask the students to identify the three main words in this verse (perfection, beauty and God). Point out Tozer's change of subject to a critique of the evangelical Church and explain that his purpose will become clear at a later point. Remind them that Tozer was critiquing the Church in the 1950s.

Our Gains and Losses

List on a board the "gains" Tozer mentions on page 178 (a simplified list is in the personal study under this subhead [*Study Guide*, p. 94]). Then compare the gains of the 1950s with our gains today. Are there others that Tozer would mention if he were here today?

No Awareness of the Eternal

1. Now list on the board the "losses" Tozer identifies on pages 178-181 (also listed in the personal study under this subhead [*Study Guide,* pp. 94-95]). Ask the class if this accurately portrays the church of today, as well as the 1950s.

2. Read Tozer's definition of worship (quoted in the personal study under this subhead [*Study Guide,* pp. 94-95]). Is this an accurate definition of worship? Based on this definition, how much worship occurs in the average church service?

External Gains, Internal Losses

Discuss with the class how external priorities relate to internal priorities in the body of Christ. Do external gains *have to* be accompanied by internal losses? How can we have both? (Help your class to come to the conclusion that focusing on one's internal relationship with God will usually result in outward growth, but that focusing on the outward result usually leads to loss—both inwardly *and* outwardly.) Introduce the next section by saying that Tozer's antidote for a loss of the sense of God's inward presence is a right view of the perfections of God.

What Is Perfection?

Ask students to propose a definition of perfection. (Refer to the personal study if they get stuck [*Study Guide,* p. 95].) Discuss Tozer's statement about perfection being "a relative word . . . that's only applied to creatures" (pp. 183-184).

No Degrees in God

1. Read for the class the first two paragraphs at the top of page 5 of the book, which explains what Tozer means by saying "there are no degrees in God." Discuss how this relates to the words "perfection" and "excellence." What is Tozer's explanation for the Bible's use of these words to refer to God?

2. Read Psalm 50:2 again. Discuss the following statement from the personal study: "All things are beautiful as they more closer to God and ugly as they move farther away" (*Study Guide*, p. 97).

What Honors God Is Beautiful

1. Ask the class what they think of Tozer's definition of theology: "the mind down on its knees in a state of breathless devotion" (*Study Guide*, p. 103). Is this their experience in thinking and learning about God?

2. Discuss Tozer's contention that we need to "rethink our whole concept of heaven" (p. 188). What are some of the wrong concepts people have of heaven? How do we bring ourselves back to a right concept of our eternal home?

Beauty Centers around Christ

Tozer says heaven is the perfection of beauty and hell is the ultimate in ugliness, with earth somewhere in between. Discuss what he means by "beauty." What is our responsibility in regard to the mix of beauty and ugliness on earth?

Nothing Bad Is Beautiful

Discuss Tozer's comment on page 191 that unholy things cannot be beautiful (quoted in the personal study under this subhead [*Study Guide*, p. 98]). How can something be "pretty," "attractive" or "charming" without being beautiful?

Nothing Wonderful in the World

Tozer implies at this point that we often get too enamored by things of the world to draw close to the Lord. What can we do to break free from our desire for things?

Closing

1. Read Tozer's prayer at the end of the chapter. Ask class members to raise their hands if they would like prayer for a fresh vision of God in His beauty.

2. Explain that next week's class will be a review of the entire book.

3. Close in prayer, remembering those who raised their hands.

Review

This lesson is designed as a review at the end of your study. The aim is simply to discern what impact the lessons have had on you (and on your students, if this is a group study) and to review the main points again.

Testimony Time

The best review might be to determine what you have gotten out of this study. If this is an individual study, write down your thoughts in a journal. If it is a group study, do it in a group discussion. Share a significant lesson the Lord has taught you or the most important thing you have learned through this study. Allow as much time as you need for this valuable exercise.

Review

Feel free to emphasize the points you feel are most needed. What is provided in this review are simply the major points each chapter made and some statements, questions or related Scriptures about each point.

Chapter 1—God's Infinitude

- "All that God is, He is without bounds or limits" (p. 4).
- Is my concept of God too small? Is it worthy of the God I serve? How would a larger view of God affect the way I live?
- Reflect on Colossians 3:1-3 in light of this quote from Tozer: "Christianity is a gateway into God. And then when you get into God, 'with Christ in God,' then you're on a journey into infinity, into infinitude. There is no limit and no place to stop" (p. 3).

Chapter 2—God's Immensity

- The man who has real faith rather than nominal faith has found a right answer to the question, "What is God like?"
- God is so immense that the universe cannot contain Him. Though He is in everything, He is not confined or contained by His creation. Instead, He contains it. Meditate on Isaiah 40.
- "You're made in the image of God, and nothing short of God will satisfy you" (p. 30). In what ways do you depend on the things of the world for your happiness? Could your faith survive the loss of all things?

Chapter 3—God's Goodness

- If God is good, He is *infinitely* good. So while we possess (in a redeemed person, at least) the ability to be good, we must not confuse that with the infinite, unchanging goodness of God.

• The ability of God to sympathize and empathize with us is found in Hebrews 2:17-18 and 4:15-16.

• "Jesus is God. And Jesus is the kindest man ever to live on this earth" (p. 52). We cannot view human kindness and hope to get an idea of what God's kindness is like. All human examples pale in comparison.

• God wants us to take pleasure in Him. Tozer's advice:"Let us put away our doubts and trust Him" (p. 55).

Chapter 4—God's Justice

• "Justice is indistinguishable from righteousness in the Old Testament" (p. 60). The Hebrew word for righteousness/justice has an implied meaning of "equal" or "equity." See Ezekiel 18:25.

• Anselm asked the question, "How dost Thou spare the wicked, if Thou art just?" Tozer says the answer to this is found in the unity of God, the passion of Christ and the unchanging nature of God.

• While punishing the wicked is just because they get what they deserve, pardoning and justifying the wicked is also just, "because it is consistent with God's nature"—God's attributes of compassion and mercy (p. 72).

Chapter 5—God's Mercy

• Tozer says mercy means "to stoop in kindness to an inferior, to have pity upon and to be actively compassionate" (p. 79) (see Psalm 103:8-17; 2 Corinthians 1:3; James 5:11; 2 Peter 3:9).

• God's mercy is an outgrowth of His goodness, His "urge to bestow blessedness" (Isaiah 63:7-9; Ezekiel 33:11).

• "Let us plunge out into the mercy of God and come to know it" (p. 95). Why? Because we need it!

Chapter 6—God's Grace

• "Grace is God's goodness confronting human demerit" (p. 98).

• Read John 1:17, then read Exodus 33:13 and 17. Did God deal with Moses on the basis of grace, or not?

• No one ever was, is or will be saved, except by grace; and grace always comes by Jesus Christ. Read Psalm 130:3.

• To know God's immeasurable grace, we must "step under the shadow of the cross" (p. 108). God's grace, released in the cross, is a mystery (1 Timothy 3:16).

Chapter 7—God's Omnipresence

• God is near to everywhere, everyone and everything; God has no borders; and God has no size (Jeremiah 23:24).

• God is always *right here*. So why do we think of Him as far away? Because our sin makes us unlike Him in our moral nature. Ephesians 2:1-3 and 4:17-19 identify this "far away" feeling as *alienation*.

- Jesus died on the cross for our sin, reconciling us to God (2 Corinthians 5:19). By putting His nature within us (2 Peter 1:4), God has removed the dissimilarity, so that we can again enjoy His conscious presence.

Chapter 8—God's Immanence

- "God dwells in His universe and yet the universe dwells in God" (p. 138). God's presence penetrates and permeates the universe (Acts 17:28).
- If God's presence penetrates and permeates the universe, why don't we sense His pervasive presence at every moment? Why are we like a man who starves to death while seated before a banquet?
- What we are yearning for is a *manifestation* of God's presence—a yearning we should *cultivate*, not ignore. This desire to be *near* God is a yearning to be *like* God. Let us not grow comfortable in our unlikeness to God, but strive to be like Christ.

Chapter 9—God's Holiness

- As fallen beings in a fallen world, "we have lost the ability to conceive of the holy" (p. 159). That is why God uses suggestion and association to describe holiness. Read Exodus 19 and look for manifestations of God that suggest or are associated with His holiness.
- We lack an awesome, awe-full respect for God's holy majesty (Psalm 50:21).
- A true vision of His holiness should cause us to live lives of repentance that we may never have

anything between us and the Holy One of Israel (Habakkuk 1:13; Lamentations 3:22; Hebrews 12:14).

Chapter 10—God's Perfection

- Read Psalm 50:2 and think through the relationship between the three prominent words in the passage: perfection, beauty and God.
- It is possible to focus on external matters to the neglect of our inner relationship with God. We spend too much time and effort on mortal things, when God wants to give us His Presence.
- All things are beautiful as they move closer to God, and ugly as they move farther away.
- "If I have a low concept of God, my religion can only be a cheap, watery affair. But if my concept of God is worthy of God then it can be noble and dignified; it can be reverent, profound, beautiful" (p. 195).

Conclusion

- This quote from chapter 3 summarizes the whole point of *The Attributes of God Volume One*:

    Christianity at any given time is strong or weak depending upon her concept of God. And I insist upon this and I have said it many times, that the basic trouble with the Church today is her unworthy conception of God. (p. 41)

- Close in prayer, asking that this study would help each person have a more worthy concept of our great and wonderful God.

More from A. W. Tozer:

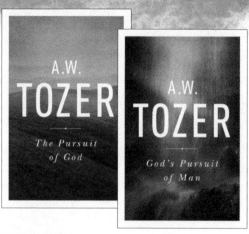

TITLES BY A.W. TOZER